The Significant Concepts of Cloud Computing

Technology, Architecture, Applications, and Security

Mohammad Samadi Gharajeh

DEDICATION

This book is dedicated to my beloved family with a special feeling of gratitude to them, to my honorable teachers for helping me to develop my technology skills, and to all researchers for their attempts to promote science.

CONTENTS

PREFACE

Everyone has an assumption about what cloud computing is. Cloud computing is a modern area emerging from distributed computing that offers many powerful benefits to different organizations. It has the ability to rent one server or thousands of servers through information technology (IT) services worldwide. The capabilities of cloud computing are gained by running a geophysical modeling application on the most powerful systems. Organizations can improve their efficiency to respond quickly and reliably to the needs of their customers. It is done through a contract for various cloud services, such as applications, software, data storage, and processing capabilities. There are some risks to cloud-based servers, such as maintaining the security of systems, asserting the privacy of information, and ensuring the rational spending of IT resources. In 2004, cloud computing progressed to public awareness. Essentially, several companies like Amazon, Google and Facebook use cloud technology as a model to run their own infrastructures. This means that dedicated services are always active, they are updated in the running systems, and the scale adapts considerably to the demand. Cloud computing involves a range of underlying technologies and configuration options rather than as a single system. Organizations must consider the strengths and weaknesses of cloud technology, service models, and implementation methods through service assessment to meet their requirements.

A cloud system can store and secure extremely large amounts of data that can only be accessed by authorized users and applications. It is endorsed and sponsored by a cloud service provider that installs a powerful platform on cloud systems. The platform involves some of the required skills, such as the operating system, Apache, a MySQL, Perl, Python and PHP database with an ability to automatically scale in response to changes in different workloads. Cloud computing can use some applications like sales automation, email, and Internet forum management. The Internet can protect data while providing consumer service, as well as it can use cloud storage to store an application, personal and business data. A cloud system with the help of the Internet can use a small number of web services to integrate maps, photos and GPS information.

This book discusses the main concepts of cloud computing. It is an appropriate tutorial for ordinary people and professionals to acquire required information about cloud technology. Chapter 1 introduces the general and fundamental characteristic of cloud systems, such as web services, grid computing and hardware virtualization. In Chapter 2, cloud computing architectures, including deployment models and defined service models for cloud-based servers, are carefully described. Chapter 3 explains various applications of cloud computing in different domains, such as file storage, cloud database, and email. In Chapter 4, some popular consumer apps designed by cloud-based systems like Evernote, iCloud, and Spotify are fully represented. Chapter 5 covers the different uses of cloud servers, such as cloud monitoring, healthcare, and banking. Chapter 6 carefully discusses cloud computing security issues, such as privacy, reliability, and compliance. Chapter 7 points out the famous simulation tools designed for cloud-based issues like CloudSim, Xen hypervisor and UEC. Finally, Chapter 8 introduces some popular companies established for cloud-based uses like CloudLock, CloudMunch, and CloudPhysics.

I hope this book can help ordinary people and professional researchers to design and implement various applications with cloud technology. Without a doubt, this book, like any product, is not without problems. Therefore, the next version of this book will be published more appropriately than the current version based on valuable suggestions from dear readers. I hope this book can help professionals to design complex systems and solve some of the existing problems. Please send any suggestions about the content of the book to my email address "mhm.samadi@gmail.com".

Mohammad Samadi Gharajeh
November 10, 2015

1 INTRODUCTION TO CLOUD COMPUTING

Cloud computing includes a relatively recent term that is the result of decades of research in grid computing, utility computing, virtualization, distributed computing, and, more recently, network services. It employs a service-oriented architecture, low overhead for end users, low cost of ownership, great flexibility, on-demand services, and many other potential capabilities. When IBM and Google declared a collaborative project in the cloud computing domain, it became more popular in October 2007. Cloud computing works on the basis of IT services similar to the Internet-oriented revolution with public access to information. It explains a popular paradigm for delivering resources and services to clients. The existing attitude implies some of the potential benefits for both cloud providers and cloud consumers. A cloud system discusses the formation of IT systems, the use of IT systems, and the organization of IT resources. The cloud has some beneficial features including virtual hardware download and associated infrastructure, instead of working only with some resources located on a single server. A virtual data center can be built quickly in bit minutes for minimal technical knowledge and the low cost of purchasing a single server.

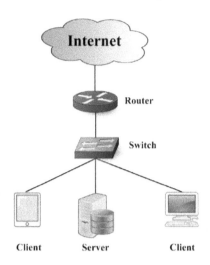

1.1 Definition

Some practical definitions for cloud computing are considered. Most web services are already called cloud services because they are often used for marketing purposes. However, a real cloud server provides some potential capabilities more than a web service. The National Institute of Standards and Technology (NIST) provides a comprehensive definition for cloud computing. It includes a useful model to enable convenient, public, and on-demand network access to a shared group of configurable computing resources, such as networks, servers, services, storage, and applications. The NIST model can be quickly and easily released and delivered with minimal management effort or low vendor interaction. A cloud system allows for economies of scale on the provider side, which significantly increases productivity in the provision of infrastructure services and improves flexibility during most problems.

1.2 The popularity feature of cloud services

Cloud services are more popular because they can reduce the cost and complexity of hiring networks and operating computers. They have some powerful benefits such as low cost, fast implementation, easy development, customization, flexible use, and compatibility with new innovations. Additionally, cloud providers that have been developed in a particular area (e.g., email, Telnet, and hosting) can provide some advanced services to customers of organizations from more than one company. The reason is that cloud users do not have to report on the IT infrastructure, buy the required hardware, and purchase software licenses. Cloud services also have other benefits for customers and users, such as scalability, reliability, and efficiency. The scalability feature of cloud computing offers unlimited storage and processing capacity. The reliability feature of cloud systems makes applications and documents accessible from anywhere in the world via the Internet. Cloud services are often efficient because they allow various organizations to update their resources according to innovations and product developments. Better protection of personal information is another benefit of cloud services. Privacy protection for cloud-based systems is enhanced by cloud computing due to the use of better security mechanisms. Meanwhile, a cloud-based server allows for more flexible IT acquisition and enhancements that allow adjustments to different procedures based on data sensitivity. Since the cloud is used in a wide variety of areas, it is possible to promote open standards for cloud computing and establish common data security across different services and providers. Information in cloud services is not easily lost compared to paper documents or hard drives.

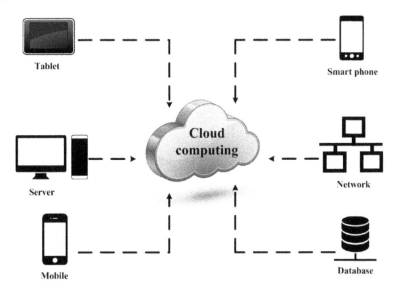

1.3 Roots of cloud computing

The roots of cloud computing can be revealed by investigating the progress of various technologies, especially in hardware (e.g., virtualization), Internet technologies (e.g., service-oriented architecture), distributed computing (e.g., grid system), and systems management (e.g., autonomic computing). These technologies have received significant attention from academia and major industry corporations. Consequently, various standardization features and modes are defined to facilitate their use in various fields and to increase the reliability and security of the systems. The emergence of cloud computing is closely related to the advancement of such technologies. A look at these technologies, which form the basic structure of cloud computing, is done in the following sections.

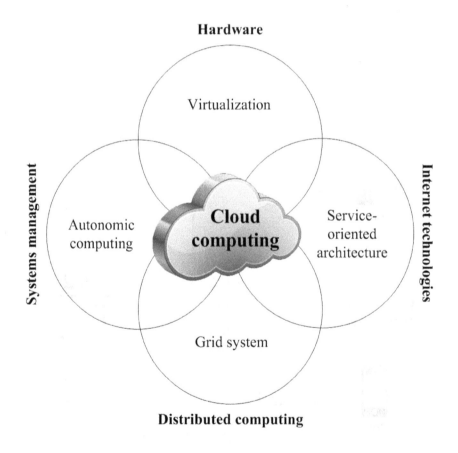

1.3.1 From mainframe to cloud

Today, the IT world changes from internally generated computers to computing resources supplied by public services that are delivered over the Internet as web services. This transformation is similar to the procedures that occurred in some famous factories a century ago, where such factories used the newly formed electrical grid instead of traditional electrical energy. It was very cheap for factories that connected their machines to new electrical energy. The on-demand response time of some popular services, such as infrastructures, business processes, and applications, through highly secure, shared, and scalable computing environments across the Internet led to the emergence of cloud computing.

This service delivery model brings potential benefits to both IT service providers and consumers. IT service providers achieve too many hiring costs by using cloud computing in their services to consumers. Multiple solutions can be provided and many users can be served by building the hardware and software infrastructures. This process increases the efficiency of services and decreases the total cost of ownership. Consumers can pay for IT-related costs lower than those paid by traditional systems by obtaining the cheapest services from external providers. The on-demand feature of this model enables consumers to tailor their IT uses to unpredictable computing needs.

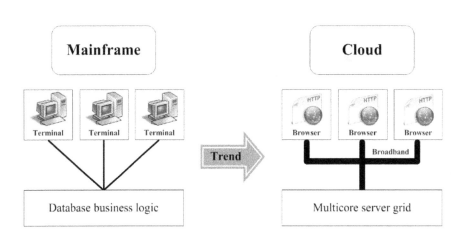

1.3.2 Web services

Web services open various network standards and have affected the advancement in the domain of software integration. The contribution of web services to each other makes web applications run on different product platforms, information is available across multiple applications, and internal applications are available on the Internet. Web services have been specified and standardized to describe various services, to carry messages between different services, and to publish web services on the Internet. Their standards have been built on existing technologies like HTTP and XML to provide a popular mechanism for delivering the service process. In addition, they lead to implementing a service-oriented architecture (SOA). An SOA determines some requirements for distributed computing that operates based on protocol-independent, standards-based, flexible docking procedures. In an SOA, resources are made up of well-defined and self-contained modules to provide business functionality, as well as a standard definition language along with an interface are used to explain services.

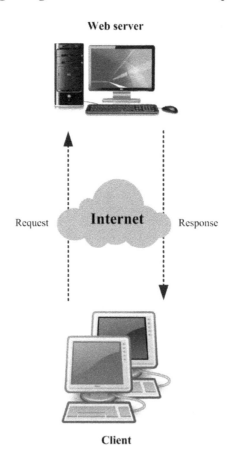

1.3.3 Grid computing

Grid computing targets distributed resources to aggregate together and access them transparently. It shares computing and storage resources across different executive domains to accelerate scientific applications such as drug design, protein analysis, and climate modeling. Web services-based protocols are created through a grid-based realization of vision to discover, allocate, and monitor distributed resources. The Open Network Services and Architecture (ONSA) achieves these purposes by defining a set of core capabilities and behaviors.

Globus toolkit is defined as a middleware to design and implement various standard grid services. It has been used to implement various infrastructures and service-oriented grid applications for several years. This toolkit presents some potential tools for collaborating with service grids (e.g., grid brokers). User interaction with multiple middleware is facilitated by such tools. Standardized protocols are developed for those activities that grid computing uses to distribute on-demand computing services over the Internet.

7

1.3.4 Utility computing

Since grid computing is a popular technology and the use of this technology has increased in the last decade, large grid systems have faced some notable problems (e.g., the need for a large amount of resources due to increase in the number of users and requests). Various techniques for managing grid resources are presented, but are not fully applicable to solving existing problems. Additionally, traditional metrics like performance, response time, and relaxation cannot meet all user requests. Therefore, there are no flexible strategies to overcome all the needs of users in grid systems.

In utility computing, users assign a utility value to their jobs to solve some problems that have occurred in grid systems. The value of the utility is a fixed or variable number that detects various restrictions for different quality of service (QoS), such as the deadline, importance and satisfaction. It is the amount of money that users require to pay a service provider to fulfill their requests. Subsequently, service providers attempt to increase utility that can directly affect profits. Users therefore compete for resource allocation according to the value of their jobs.

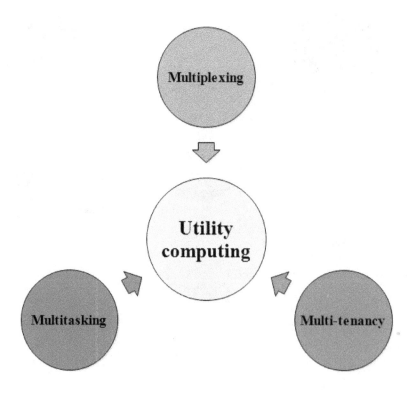

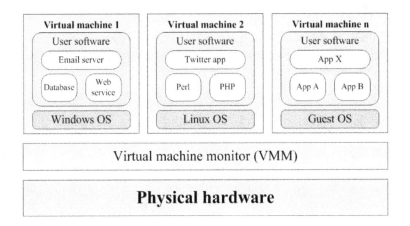

1.3.5 Hardware virtualization

Hardware virtualization in cloud computing is generally used by large-scale data centers involving thousands of computers. Such large-scale centers serve many users around the world (e.g., companies) and host many diverse platforms (e.g., computational applications). Due to some problems in the operational and maintenance uses of data centers, hardware virtualization can be applied to overcome these problems. The virtualization process of a computer is performed for various resources such as processors, memory, and I/O devices to share and use computer systems in various areas. Multiple operating systems and software applications can be run on a single physical platform using hardware virtualization. Software layers are placed inside virtual machines (VMs) that are virtual platform interfaces. They have access to physical hardware through a virtual machine monitor (VMM), called a hypervisor.

1.4 General characteristics of cloud computing

Cloud computing, compared to other services, has some characteristics in both aspects of advantages and disadvantages. Due to its growth in various fields and areas, most companies increase financial investments to serve their customers with cloud computing. Cloud systems allow organizations to focus on their competencies with other companies in an appropriate way. They allow the use of evolutionary processes in IT problems, use great complexity in web-based systems, and improve the concealment of information. Unnecessary details will be hidden to serve users, as well as some key parameters, which are necessary for the core business, are easily controlled by cloud devices. The general features of cloud computing include remote data centers, pooling of resources, infinite scalability, pay per use, and self service.

Remote data centers mean that high-level data centers provide cloud services to end users and their institutions through Internet services. Data centers often use cheap electronic sources in a way that their users do not know their location. Cloud providers generally determine which data centers are appropriate for user requests. In some cases, users may require those of the services found in special countries with different capacities and security.

Pooling of resources means that multiple clients, such as data warehousing, processors, and bandwidths, are shared among clients anywhere in the world. They are dynamically assigned to different customer requests regarding their demands. When a problem occurs in the hardware components of the data centers, those components are replaced with new hardware without affecting the availability or efficiency of the system. Cloud system resources can be used across multiple data centers to provide greater security and resiliency.

Infinite scalability is one of the important features of cloud computing, so data centers can be easily expanded based on new demands. On the other hand, it is a key feature of cloud systems that allows for sudden peaks in demand. When a cloud institution needs to increase its service capabilities, the upgrade process will take place during a short time. However, cloud scalability often refers to the hardware reconfiguration of cloud systems.

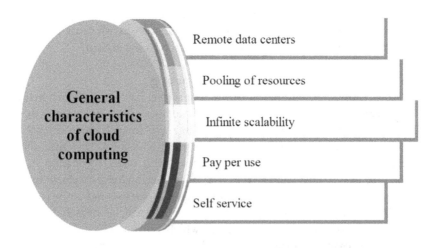

General characteristics of cloud computing

- Remote data centers
- Pooling of resources
- Infinite scalability
- Pay per use
- Self service

Pay per use of cloud services means that customers pay certain costs depending on the terms of service required for cloud applications and resources. These costs are paid to cloud service providers that offer cloud services to their customers. The prices of the services depend on some parameters, such as the time of service, QoS and the type of service (e.g., scientific purposes). However, distributed cloud centers allow providers to offer uniform pricing strategies without regard to any additional parameters.

Self service in cloud computing means customers can select their desired hardware resources and software applications. Additionally, customers can increase or decrease any resource without discussion with the assigned cloud provider. They can monitor the amount of resource usage with some reporting facilities that are provided by cloud hubs. Reporting capabilities allow clients to obtain the necessary information about contracted resources.

1.5 Special characteristics and benefits

In addition to general features, each technology has some special features and benefits that make it apart from other technologies. The specific business expectations of a technology are necessarily related to its particular circumstances. Cloud computing has some specific characteristics and benefits, including innovation speed, availability, economic efficiency, scalability, elasticity, and efficiency.

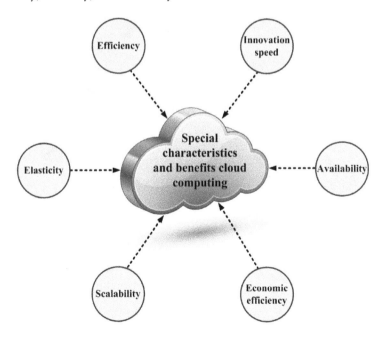

1.5.1 Innovation speed

Cloud systems can be delivered and scaled up in just a few hours in contrast to traditional IT systems that were deployed over several weeks or months. A cloud system provides a quick and easy way to design and implement business processes. Furthermore, it finds new ways to interact with customers. Cloud computing offers a new platform for the kind of technical experimentation, rapid development, and easy deployment that IT departments use. A company can quickly fulfill multiple requests from its customers using cloud services. It responds to changes of available products as fast as possible. A system implemented by cloud technology can be faster because it has three important characteristics, such as linking current systems with next generation systems, involving a foundation for a flexible assembly model, and automating services in a hybrid cloud environment.

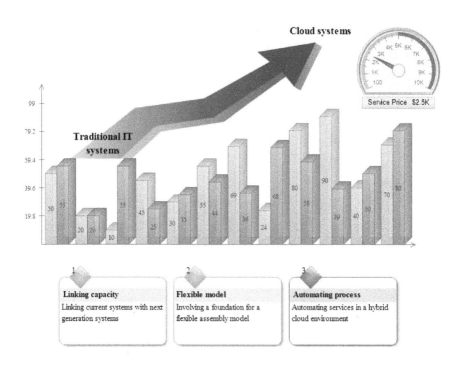

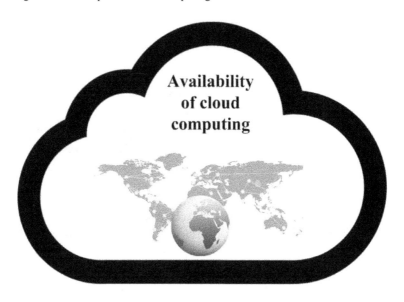

1.5.2 Availability

Because cloud providers have great capacity to scale in a distributed environment, they can offer high availability to customers. A cloud server achieves high availability for business requirements through redundant interconnection and load balancing. Therefore, the degree of availability of a service provider must be measured by an independent external entity. The availability of cloud systems implies the idea of access to services, tools and data anytime, anywhere. It is also related to the characteristic reliability of data centers. A service can have high availability if it is always activated and has high reliability. In addition, hosting services at multiple providers located in different positions reduces the probability of failure.

1.5.3 Economic efficiency

Organizations do not invest a large amount of cost to build and maintain their own IT infrastructures using cloud computing with scalable capacity. This process makes desired services and capabilities available on demand and pay-as-use. By using this capability in cloud services, organizations do not have to pay for the costs of their internal resources that customers do not use frequently. They can save much more money to drive innovation in their core business instead of dissipating money on unused infrastructure. Therefore, current IT costs and potential cloud solution prices must be paid by organizations.

Traditional IT systems **Cloud systems**

1.5.4 Scalability

The flexibility and scalability features of cloud systems allow cloud systems to quickly adapt to IT infrastructures to change business needs in different conditions. Therefore, IT systems with the help of cloud computing can better meet and support business requirements. It reacts quickly and automatically to operate according to user requirements due to the high degree of availability of services. Using the scalability feature of cloud services, it can allocate various resources (e.g., data files and hardware) as needed. Meanwhile, existing resources can be upgraded to high hardware capacities through low maintenance costs during a short runtime to respond to new user demands.

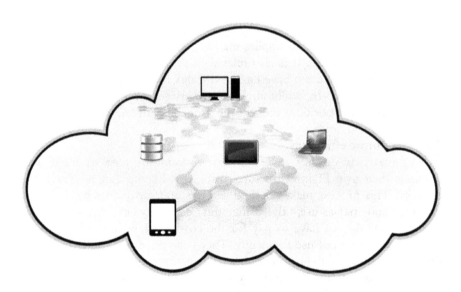

1.5.5 Elasticity

The elasticity term is widely used in cloud computing in vast aspects of physics and economics. It is commonly known as the ability of a cloud system for automatic on-demand provisioning and de-provisioning of computing resources as workloads change. Current definitions of cloud elasticity are largely inconsistent and nonspecific, leading to confusion in the use of related terms such as scalability and efficiency. A technical definition of cloud elasticity can be achieved by the ability to increase the stable degree of data centers against different natural problems. The cloud service provider has some duplicate systems that can be used for both disaster recovery and load balancing situations. Electronic resources in the cloud can be protected against natural disasters by considering the geographical separation in the server rooms.

1.5.6 Efficiency

An organization can focus on its main business programs and can invest in research and development through innovative ways. The efficiency of cloud computing helps an organization to make a substantial contribution. A company can optimize efficiency by enabling the provision of a continuous service to its customers on a cloud platform. Cloud computing necessarily provides some business capabilities to cloud providers to increase their accountability to customers. Some factors can improve the efficiency of a service provider, such as increasing the number of successful jobs, decreasing execution time, and reducing hiring costs.

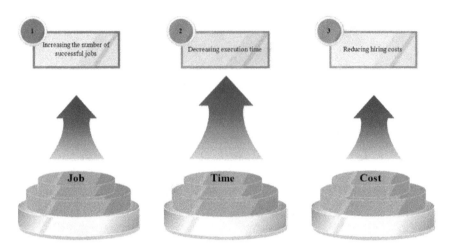

1.6 The IT foundation for cloud systems

The cloud computing infrastructure is built by some underlying pieces of technology. It is an extended version of traditional IT systems to respond to customer requests through web-based tools. The underlying pieces for building cloud systems include infrastructure, IP-based networks, virtualization, software, and service interfaces.

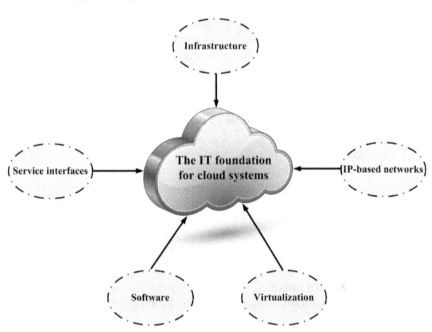

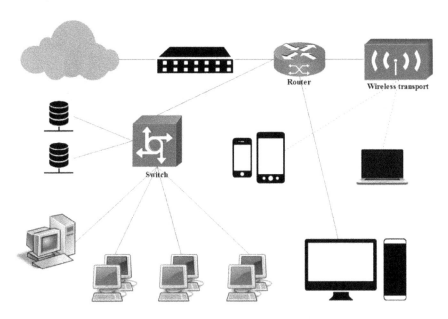

1.6.1 Infrastructure

The cloud computing infrastructure consists of several elements, including computer servers, storage disks, and network components. These elements are organized together to allow cloud systems to grow incrementally well beyond typical scale-level infrastructure. They must be chosen for their capabilities to support some requirements for efficiency, scalability, robustness and security. Known business servers may not offer the appropriate reliability, network support, or other qualities to deliver various services efficiently and securely to users. Meanwhile, cloud servers can operate on less expensive hardware and can be more accurate without internal storage disks on each server.

1.6.2 IP-based networks

In the cloud server infrastructure, the network connects a large number of users located in different locations to the cloud systems. In addition, the network interconnects the internal cloud servers with each other. An enterprise network model cannot meet the current needs for efficient and secure cloud operations. In cloud systems, the network requires disk operation to determine carrier-level network capacity along with some optimized network strategies. Keep in mind that multiple switches in data paths between cloud servers become single points of failure and high costs through various network issues.

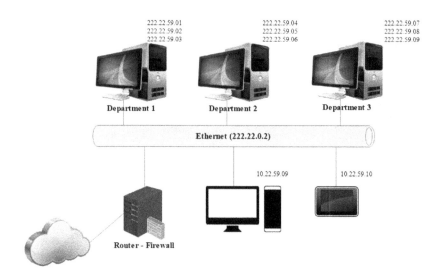

1.6.3 Virtualization

Virtualization is used in cloud computing, so a single physical server is divided into multiple VMs and a single physical resource (e.g., storage and networking) is dedicated to multiple tasks. It allows to build the server consolidation with great flexibility of use. Additionally, virtualization is used in cloud computing for rapid commissioning and decommissioning of servers. Multipurpose software is implemented for cloud virtualization to offer a dynamic perspective and a unified aspect of resource utilization. This is efficient for cloud uses in IT operations. With the help of virtualization capabilities, cost-effective server utilization is achieved during media separation between multiple populations on physical hardware.

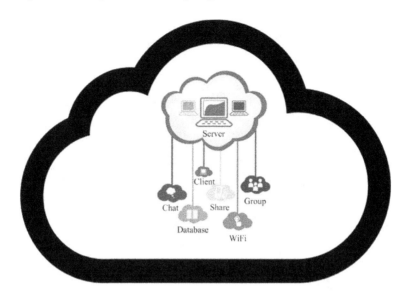

1.6.4 Software

A dedicated software platform enables all the capabilities of cloud computing, such as infrastructure management, service development, provisioning, accounting, and security. The cloud server infrastructure dynamically enforces policies for some purposes, including separation, isolation, monitoring, and service composition. Cloud software is enabled by some regular cloud infrastructure patterns to automate the tasks required for the elasticity function. It is accomplished to provide services to customers using servers, VMs, disk warehouses, services, and other IT components. In fact, provisioning and deprovisioning processes can be automated by software in the cloud.

1.6.5 Service interfaces

A primary differentiator for cloud computing is the service interface between cloud providers and consumers. The service interface explains a contract to enforce the value proposition with price terms. It makes cloud servers stand out as new. Additionally, it creates some competitive values and enables competition between cloud service providers. Self-service interfaces get some additional optimizations. Cloud customers can contract cloud resources (e.g., disk storage) through an automated process without using IT systems. The graphical interfaces are designed to express storage and other resources to cloud users to define virtual IT infrastructures. Keep in mind that some professional tools can build your own virtual data center, like a web browser and a credit card.

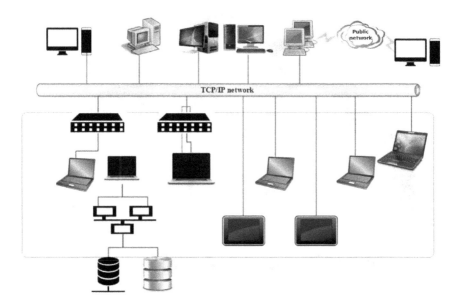

1.7 Risks of cloud computing

Cloud computing is a new technology that is used for some purposes in various institutions. It performs computer services requested by a large number of clients located in different organizations. In addition, executive directors of institutions may feel uncomfortable when transferring business data hosting and service teams. Therefore, some risks with perception may be more possible than those with reality. From one point of view, the risks of cloud computing are classified into three groups, including data security, unwanted advertising and lock-in.

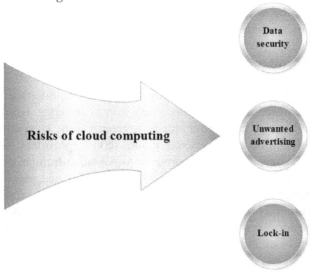

Data security: Organizations and companies may consider their data to be more secure if they are housed within their local warehouses. Transferring data to external warehouses for hosting in remote data centers, which are not under the control of organizations and in locations that may not be popular or reliable, presents a significant risk. Cloud providers determine some guarantees required in their contracts with customers that personal data will only be stored on private servers. The main risk is that there may be a breach of confidentiality that involves a staff member appealing to high-cost organizations. Since high service availability is one of the main benefits of cloud servers, there are some threat risks, such as denial of service attacks against data storage. Most risks can be minimized by using multiple cloud service providers instead of using a single cloud service provider.

Unwanted advertising: Sending unsolicited email or advertising to customers from cloud providers is another risk for cloud systems. Because there are a large number of penalties for infringements, cloud servers should not do unwanted advertising. Therefore, service providers must offer some guarantees required in the contract with customers so that unsolicited email or advertising is eliminated considerably. It causes the popularity rate of cloud servers to increase in several areas.

Lock-in: Some companies like Microsoft and Google allow organizations to make multiple brands for their cloud products. It can lead to risk by associating an organization with such companies whose popularity varies among customers. However, a greater risk is that an organization will crash products from a particular supplier. There are a lot of costs to migrate from widely used systems to other systems. Because some cloud service providers make claims on the various providers of their products, it is easy to transfer data from one system to another.

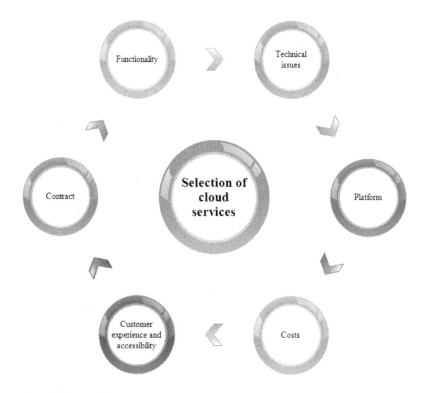

1.8 Selection of cloud services

Most institutions have the idea that cloud services can provide a list of selection criteria so that they can compete together on the response side to their clients. In one view, cloud service selection procedures are categorized into six characteristics, including functionality, technical issues, platform, costs, customer experience and accessibility, and contract.

Functionality: A cloud service must include the functionality required by users. In the case of email, the required functionality may involve the use of a POP client instead of a web-based platform. In this case, messages outside the office can be displayed to clients when they are on vacation. In the case of document storage, the usages considered may imply the allocation of total space per user and the various types of files that can be stored. In the case of office applications, file compatibility may be the functionality required in a particular topic. This case is often used when documents are created using cloud software and can be viewed using different cloud provider applications in the future. The functionality is also useful for evaluating the level of the integration process between different applications that are provided within a set of products.

Technical issues: The institution, which supports its clients with a cloud service, may not perform some technical integration work. Automating the creation of user accounts on a cloud system and facilitating single sign-on to systems are some of these jobs. In addition, monitoring usage, deleting user accounts, and performing system administration activities are other essential tasks.

Platform: The platforms in the applications, which are provided by cloud services, must be carefully evaluated. In an ideal state, the software will work the same across all devices, operating systems, and web browsers. It may be necessary for users to be advised to use particular platforms. Furthermore, access to cloud servers via mobile devices has become increasingly essential for many students.

Costs: Institutions consider the real costs for contracting cloud services. In addition, minimum or non-existent prices may appear. The costs of any legal advice can be estimated with contractual negotiations, project management and technical integration. The minimum costs to contract the cloud capabilities by an institution are related to different parameters, such as the type of service and the requirements of the users.

Customer experience and accessibility: Some of the cloud services offer a better customer experience and accessibility to the source than others. The usability of cloud platforms is an important and necessary requirement to install additional software in the web browser. The software must be more attractive to customers. The use of the software by some disabled users is required to be considered for ethical and legal reasons. Because institutions want to implement cloud services, they must ensure confirmation of the software against web-based guidelines and standards.

Contract: The cloud provider has a standard contract that needs to be investigated closely. Famous and large organizations are at great risk, so they need legal advice before signing the contract with cloud providers. There are some issues that need to be accurately assessed in terms of the initial contract step, early withdrawal penalties, and possible future costs. The service-level agreement (SLA) can provide the organization with payment in case of service interruption. For free cloud services, payment may be limited to the provision of the contract extensions. Therefore, these services can provide little security to clients who can be guided to discuss with other clients about the services in the process of implementation. When an institution presents cheap or free services, it must offer direct assistance to the client. Therefore, most high-level cloud services require a minimal support system.

1.9 The difference between Web 2.0 and cloud computing

Some people think that cloud computing refers to any service provider over the Internet that their organization does not consider. Therefore, there is confusion between the terms of Web 2.0 and cloud computing. When cloud computing emerged, there was disagreement over the exact meaning of Web 2.0. Some of the social networks are generally developed as Web 2.0 applications. They allow their users to change the content of web pages and interact with other users. Such software may be hosted by an organization or it may be accessible via the Internet. It can be accessed through cloud services with various features, such as fast elasticity and pay-per-use. Web 2.0 can be considered as a particular type of applications. In contrast, cloud computing is a method used by such applications with the help of some data hosted and delivered to users.

1.10 Policy implications

There are several important policy implications of cloud computing in terms of education, regional issues, and international levels. The functions of computing processes involve from the provision of cloud services to the monitoring of these services and some network relationships with cloud providers. Employees of an institution oversee the landscape developed by cloud servers and organize in advance for the restoration of cloud service contracts. Institutions must provide data security for their services and manage existing risks by entering into security contracts with cloud providers. In addition, they must allow their clients to bypass institutional policies on computer distribution.

The ownership of the data must be determined within the contract. Cloud service contracts must state that customers retain ownership of the data supplied by cloud storage. Educational organizations may want to designate the ownership of customers who upload content from the cloud. New mental property rights are clearly realized when educational materials are stored in cloud stores. Contractual arrangements for cloud services obtained by regional educational authorities are better performed than those obtained by individual institutions. These institutions (e.g., smaller schools, colleges, and universities) cannot obtain expensive legal services.

2 CLOUD COMPUTING ARCHITECTURE

A cloud computing system is generally divided into two sections that include the front end and the back end. They are connected to each other through a network (e.g., the Internet). The front end is the client side (e.g., customers) and the back end is the cloud section of the system. In a technical view, the architecture of cloud computing is classified into two groups, including deployment models and service models.

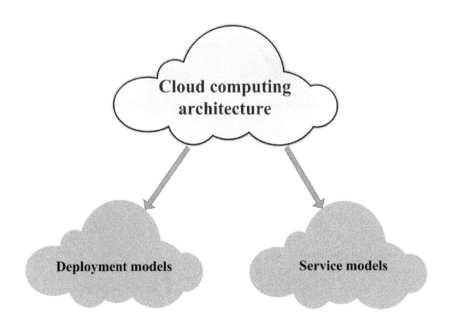

2.1 Deployment models

IT institutions can deploy their applications in public, private, hybrid or community clouds. These models do not dictate cloud server locations. However, public clouds are generally located on the Internet and private clouds are generally located on private networks related to each institution. Organizations may have a number of interests related to the cloud computing model they select to employ, as well as they may use more than one cloud model to solve different problems. An ordinary or temporary application may be suitable for deployment in a public cloud due to the lack of need to purchase additional equipment. Similarly, a permanent or technical application may be suitable for deployment in a private or hybrid cloud due to the need to purchase additional requirements such as QoS and data location.

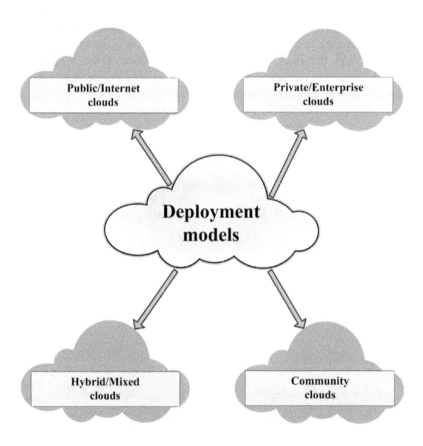

2.1.1 Public clouds

Public clouds are used to run temporary or general applications that are requested from all clients without the need for additional equipment. In these types of computing models, the applications of different clients are mixed in the servers, storage media and cloud networks. Public clouds are generally hosted far from customer locations. They reduce the risks and costs of customers using a flexible and temporary extension to the business infrastructure. If a public cloud is designed and implemented with performance, data location, and security in mind, other applications must run in the cloud transparently for both cloud architects and end users. Having a larger capacity than a company's private cloud, offering the ability to scale with respect to demands and shifting infrastructure risks from enterprise to cloud provider are some of the potential benefits of public clouds.

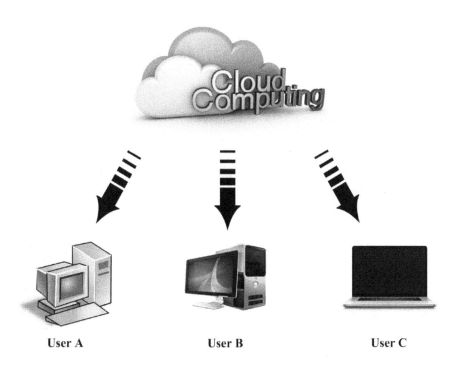

| User A | User B | User C |

2.1.2 Private clouds

Private clouds are designed and implemented for the exclusive use of a client. They provide additional control over data, security, and QoS. An institution purchases a business infrastructure so that it has some powerful controls over how various applications are implemented in it. This type of computing model can be built and managed by an IT organization or a cloud service provider. An organization can install, configure and operate its own infrastructure to support the private cloud. Providing a high level of control over the use of cloud resources to organizations to establish and operate their experience environment is one of the most important benefits of private clouds.

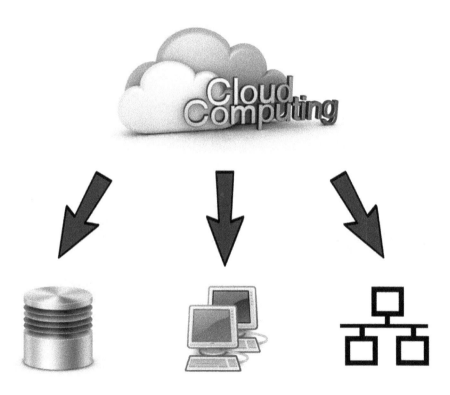

2.1.3 Hybrid clouds

Hybrid clouds integrate public and private cloud deployment models. They provide on-demand and external scales for special uses. The ability to scale a private cloud with the resources available from a public cloud can be used to maintain service levels in the face of rapid workload alternations. The use of storage clouds can often be provided to support Web 2.0 applications. Meanwhile, some planned workload spikes can be handled by a hybrid cloud. Hybrid clouds can determine the complexity of the applications that will be distributed in a public and private cloud. A hybrid cloud can run multiple applications with the relationship between data and processing resources. A hybrid cloud for small data or stateless applications can be much more successful than a public cloud for large amounts of data and a small number of processing uses.

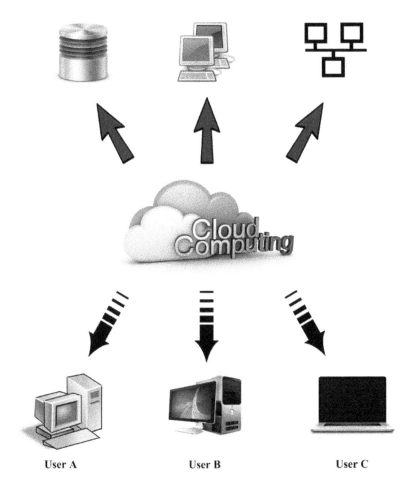

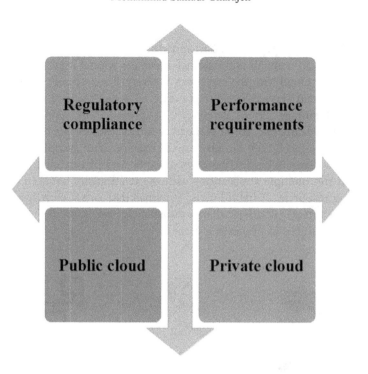

2.1.4 Community clouds

A community cloud is a multi-tenant infrastructure that can be shared among multiple institutions in a special group for common computing purposes. These purposes may be related to regulatory compliance (e.g., auditing requirements) or may be related to performance requirements (e.g., hosting applications required for fast response time). Organizations can realize the benefits of a public cloud (e.g., multi-tenancy and a pay-as-you-go billing structure) with the additional levels of privacy, security, and policy compliance that are often associated with a private cloud. Keep in mind that a community cloud can be local or external.

2.2 Service models

Service models represent what type of services a cloud system can support. They are classified into three main groups: Infrastructure as a Service (IaaS), Platform as a Service (PaaS) and Software as a Service (SaaS). Cloud providers offer different services related to the selected model. Such services are generally grouped with respect to the level of the IT architecture. In a practical sense, these groups are offered by cloud service providers to a large number of clients.

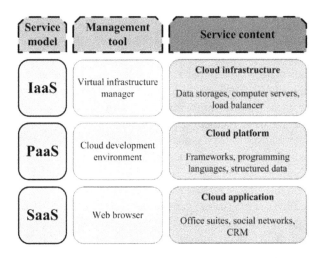

2.2.1 IaaS model

Virtualized on-demand resources (e.g., computing, data storage, and communication) can be provided by a cloud system like the IaaS model. A cloud infrastructure enables on-demand servers that can run multiple operating systems and custom software platforms. Such services are the bottom layer of cloud computing systems. Amazon Web Services often provides IaaS by offering VMs with a software stack through their EC2 service. This software can be customized in a similar way to an ordinary physical server. Users have privileges to perform various activities on the server, such as starting the server, stopping the server, installing the necessary software packages, connecting virtual disks to the server, configuring access permissions, and defining firewall rules.

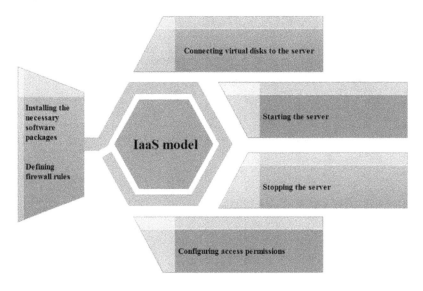

2.2.2 PaaS model

In addition to infrastructure-based clouds that offer raw computing and data storage services, the second service model provides a higher level of abstraction to create a rapidly programmable cloud environment, known as PaaS. On this cloud platform, developers and programmers design and deploy applications without knowing how many processors and how many memory chips are used in their applications. Meanwhile, such applications involve some building blocks consisting of multiple programming models and various specialized cloud services (e.g., data access, authentication, and payments). Google App Engine is an instance of the PaaS model that provides a scalable framework for creating and developing web-oriented applications. These applications can be developed in specific programming languages (e.g., Python and Java). They are made up of basic components that consist of mail service, instant messaging service (XMPP), in-memory object cache (Memcache) and integration with the Google authentication service.

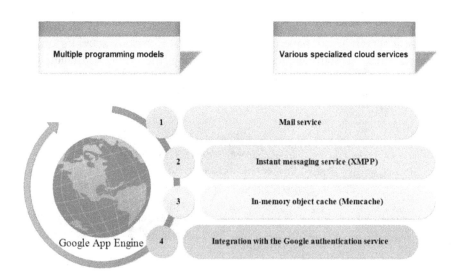

2.2.3 SaaS model

Applications have taken the top level of the cloud stack. End users can access the services provided by this layer through web portals. Therefore, consumers at various institutions increasingly migrate from local computing platforms to online software services with the same functionality. This model of cloud application delivery is called SaaS. The burden of software maintenance for organizations' customers will be reduced and this model will facilitate development and testing capacity for cloud providers. Traditional desktop applications (e.g., word processing and spreadsheet) may currently be available as a service in web environments.

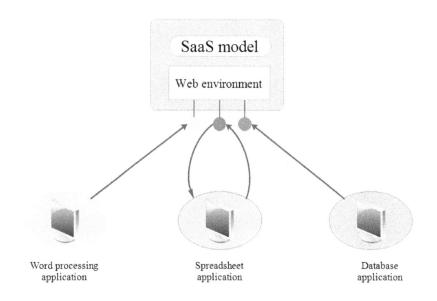

3 CLOUD COMPUTING APPLICATIONS

Over the past decade, large organizations consider cloud computing to support their clients for various applications, such as sales services, scientific projects, and file uses. Some of these applications are very important to such organizations and others are medium importance. This chapter explains the most common cloud computing applications.

3.1 File storage and sharing

Nowadays, sending and receiving very large files by email is one of the main requirements of people. Some of the services like SendFile, Dropbox and JungleDisk meet this requirement for years. Apple advises industrial companies to describe cloud computing concepts to the general population. Since 2012, people are empowered with some mature and powerful options for secure file sharing for workgroups, team collaboration, and file storage. There is no need to stream large attachments from cloud drive to hosted SharePoint. Any partner and client of cloud systems can have a place on cloud servers to share information and documents.

3.2 Cloud database

Every web application requires a database at all times. In recent years, web developers and researchers have used some of the popular databases, such as Microsoft Access, MySQL, and Microsoft SQL Server. Therefore, they have to use highly technical skills to perform complex tasks and to manage and support a database. Previously, these tasks could be performed by a database administrator. Today, developers use powerful and scalable database files to make the complex tasks that cloud database tools provide easier. Everything can be monitored and investigated as a service by a cloud database. Rackspace provides various database functions through a cloud-based web application.

3.3 CRM

A large number of companies use cloud computing for mission critical applications. Customer Relationship Management (CRM) systems are one of those applications that address two more sensitive types of data, including customer information and revenue. Until now, most institutions would not like to host their CRM applications on-premises. Some of the famous companies (e.g., Salesforce) have exponentially increased their business services through cloud servers. The powerful benefits of cloud-based CRM systems are obvious to purchasing groups. Meanwhile, potential risks have also been addressed by such business groups. CRM applications can transfer more lines of business applications to cloud environments.

3.4 Email

Email is another instance of web-based applications, which is matured and standardized. It can also be moved from traditional servers to cloud environments. International institutions, which provide email services to their users, need to transfer their existing email services to cloud-based servers as soon as possible. Today, we use cloud-based consumer email services (e.g., Gmail and Hotmail) to enjoy the benefits of access to letters anywhere without having to think about the capacity or time of server activity. There are some potential cloud-based email services for any business to be hosted as low-cost email, hosted as an exchange for small businesses, and managed as dedicated exchange environments for large customers.

3.5 PaaS for web applications

The PaaS service model was adapted to a well-known word in 2011. It is considered an overhyped cloud service model. A PaaS allows designers and developers to host their dedicated applications without having any technical information about their servers. Developers only need to upload their applications to cloud-based systems. The caution is that the "stack" app is a black box that has predefined some components and settings. It provides ideal PaaS, similar to cloud sites, for independent web developers, microsites, and standalone applications. Such applications have no need to stack customizations and have no interaction with other trading platforms.

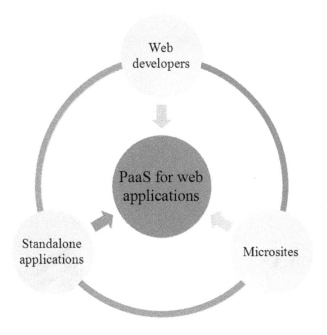

3.6 File backup

Someone is needed to back up essential files and documents. In fact, a small number of people perform backup operations consistently and efficiently. Until recently, files were backed up to disk or tape. But now, a robust backup keeps a copy of files and documents on a remote server. Therefore, files must be sent from traditional media to stable storage that is logistically complex, slow, and inexpensive. Cloud-based storage is a potential solution for automatically backing up information based on a predefined schedule. In cloud-based systems, files and documents are stored on a secure remote server where it can be available when needed.

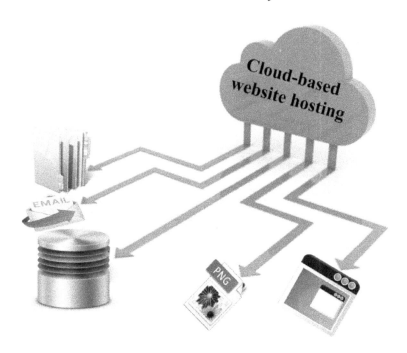

3.7 Website hosting

If a website is visited frequently, you may have a great loss of traditional IT resources. Web providers can create the best web content by hosting their websites on cloud servers that are combined with existing managed services. Cloud-based web hosting capabilities offer great scalability and high availability for different sites, from a simple web blog to high traffic commercial websites. In addition, this type of web hosting has a high security against the different Internet-based risks.

3.8 E-commerce

Availability, scalability, and security are essential factors for Internet-based stores. A low-speed store site can lead to customer loss. E-commerce is used to facilitate online sales capabilities. Cloud computing enables online stores to dynamically sell their products with the help of some powerful infrastructure. When a problem occurs on an e-commerce website, the management system can slow down traditional servers to prevent customers from making a purchase. Note that cloud-based servers allow the same website to quickly accelerate additional resources to handle the upload process. In addition, cloud systems allow the deployment of web servers in different locations. This process speeds up the loading times of a local page and increases the availability of the website considerably.

3.9 Development and test

A software corporation may implement business software or develop software applications for sale as products in online markets. Therefore, it requires some environments that involve a configuration of servers, storage and networks. Software development teams can create such environments on cloud servers instead of buying and maintaining traditional IT servers. This process causes multiple instances of an application to be created in minutes and the product purchase process to be efficient. Moreover, additional software instances can be used for testing and learning purposes with the same performance. Additionally, cloud-based processes can test and simulate the upload process under different hardware configurations.

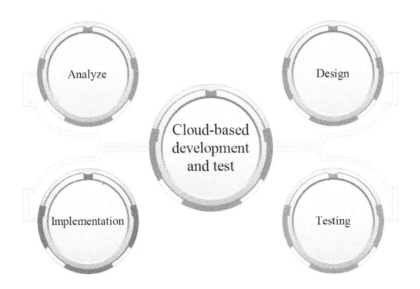

3.10 Private and hybrid clouds

Private clouds offer many benefits of public clouds that use an isolated network and computing resources to provide additional security. Rackspace provides private clouds to give IT departments many controls. These controls are carried out on resources and architectures. Hybrid clouds are provided to allow IT departments to connect public clouds, private clouds, dedicated hosts, and on-premise infrastructures to provide an efficient combination of control and agility. A web server can be installed in a public cloud, transaction processing can be done on a dedicated server, and the ordering process can be done in a private cloud.

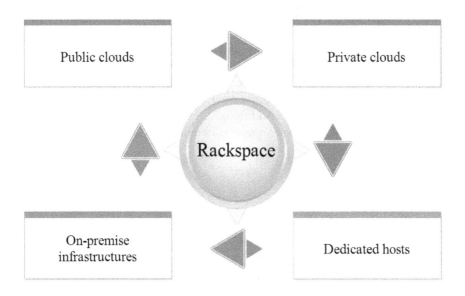

4 CONSUMER CLOUD APPLICATIONS

During the last decade, cloud computing has been considered as a technical field in various applications. Unlike the Internet, a cloud-based server is a unique network of interconnected resources. These servers can be used for sales purchases, scientific operations, etc. This chapter covers some of the consumer applications that can be deployed using cloud systems.

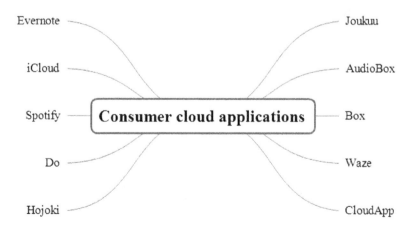

4.1 Evernote

Evernote does one thing to perform the dedicated operations very well. It collects multiple data clips from the websites you are reading or the applications you are using. Additionally, Evernote collects them into different categories that can be synced in the cloud environment and can be accessed from multiple devices. Several collections of the applications have been extended to many students. Today, laptops, tablets, and desktop computers at some universities are the primary research tools for all academic uses. Evernote has rapidly increased to the level of ubiquity among such technical classes of users. It is a web-based application that allows end users to capture, store and synchronize various files such as text, image and video on multiple computing devices. Evernote can improve your life through various ways, including keeping track of your time, writing a note to your partner, journaling, book notes, collaborating at work, gift ideas, shopping list, saving articles, and other interesting things for later, saving your clothing size and useful measurements, goal tracking, digital rolodex, financial tracking, meal and diary master list, fitness/weight journal, writing a book, sending voice notes, record interviews or other important meetings, master to-do list, distraction to-do list, honey-do list, keep information and phone numbers for your insurance policy, itinerary and vacation information handy, the wish list, class/meeting notes, pocket notebook, organizing resources, remind yourself of things you want to do, record daily projects you would like to do, learn your family history and common book.

4.2 iCloud

The establishment of Apple's platform on devices and services is deliberate, systematic and brilliant. iCloud can be considerable for not having been a spectacular failure. The main brilliance of Apple's marketing services is that iCloud has no direct competition with Android. What services Android lacks and what services iCloud provides is a description of the service as an ever-present resource that is connected to the iPhone, iPad and Mac. iCloud is another capability that can run an Apple device. iCloud Drive is one of several ways to store, sync, and update files and documents between your Apple devices. Apple has updated its cloud-based storage system to make it more available and visible to many third-party users and technical developers. In fact, iCloud connects you and your Apple devices in surprising ways. This ability can access the latest versions of the most important things (e.g., photos, documents, applications, notes and contacts) anywhere you are using your Apple devices. It allows you to quickly share photos, calendars, locations, and more with your friends and family.

4.3 Spotify

Spotify is a Swedish ownership-oriented music streaming service that lets you instantly listen to special music tracks or albums without buffering delay time. It makes it easy to search for music by artist, album, record label, created playlists and direct searches. The service provided by Spotify can be freely downloaded by anyone. Currently, you need to sign up for an account to receive an invitation from an existing member.

Some streams between songs and commercials will be shown in the main window when you are using the free version of Spotify. Note that the free version of the service is only accessible in some countries, including Norway, Sweden, Great Britain, France and Spain. Spotify offers its services through three types, including free, unlimited, and premium. Everyone who purchases a premium member account can give access to all songs without commercial interruptions.

4.4 Do

Do involves various levels and efforts of file sharing functionality and collaboration service. It includes those of the capabilities that have already been attached to Outlook through some plugins, but are not accessible to regular Outlook users. Salesforce is squeezing out from under Outlook and threatening home users and small business users by linking Do to Gmail as their primary message service. Although Do may indent Hosted Exchange services for smaller companies, but it may not be a threat to Exchange. In addition, Do helps any team manage various projects and tasks. It is a set of project management tools for professional uses and can be manipulated to customize it to meet the needs of any business. Do offers various capabilities, such as managing single/multiple project, managing different people, managing groups of people, having full mobility for a team, having a favorite calendar tool, integrating directly with Google account, and referring to various Gmail gadgets.

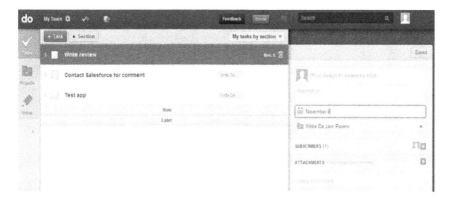

4.5 Hojoki

A large number of industries are built around the world, which are called collaboration platforms. They allow the necessary capabilities to share documents and files between different members of their teams. There are several individual cloud-based applications (e.g., Beanstalk, Dropbox, and Evernote) that work based on some individual tasks. One of their limited situations is that they are handled independently and are not linked to each other. Hojoki is produced to obtain a linking function to such individual applications. It builds a flow of people who can share contacts and are able to organize into different groups for collaborative projects. Possible activities within the group are channeled through the Hojoki sequence to members so that the application is an automatic monitor of the progress of the task. Hojoki includes several features, such as integrating any favorite productivity application, creating multiple projects, inviting an unlimited number of team members, defining shared elements in each project, status messages, involved labels of connected applications, magic search, magic filtering, real-time notification and filtering news feed for people.

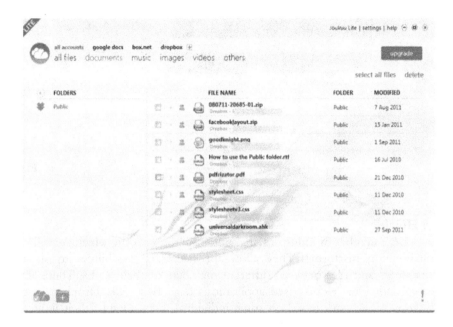

4.6 Joukuu

The content of files and documents stored on cloud servers (e.g., Google Docs, Microsoft SkyDrive, and Dropbox) can be displayed in a single list using a web-based console. When you work with a large number of colleagues on an individual project and all workers subscribe to different services, Joukuu will help you save time considerably. This app has an out-of-browser app that allows you to use drag and drop functionality instead of a thousand clicks per day. It will reduce the time required for a project and improve work efficiency. Joukuu includes various capabilities, such as supporting multiple accounts, searching the file between accounts, sharing files easily and safely, editing files in Google Docs, collaborating with other people and having a desktop application.

4.7 AudioBox

There are many services in the world that offer some storage mechanisms for your music collections on cloud-based servers. They allow you to access music collections from anywhere. In recent years, AudioBox has been a major reboot application with an appropriate procedure to bring everything to the cloud-based music table. This app is a streaming service that grants requirements anyway. People can store all the music they own in the cloud-based spaces, as well as can play music from any device using the multimedia player dedicated to the service application.

AudioBox constantly consists of the appropriate improvements and various enhancements to be the best web application around us. It involves more features like accessing your favorite music from anywhere, playing music without downloading a desktop media player, listening to your favorite songs anywhere, and preventing loss of downloaded music in the event of a hard drive crash.

4.8 Box

Social networks (e.g., Facebook and LinkedIn) help you get in touch with various people around the world. Although LinkedIn is a social area, it is also a professional and business-oriented environment. But, like most social media, it is not a suitable place to store and share a large number of files and documents. Box is designed to solve this problem. The latest web-based platform designed for this application works with any browser. It allows you to store and manage all your files and documents online and quickly. Through Box, anyone can manage content intuitively, share files securely, and work together easily. It allows you to choose, get quick and easy access to documents, project plans, presentations and multimedia. This application can be run on different platforms like iPhone, iPad and Android. It has some additional capabilities, like syncing files to your desktop, running office applications, getting rid of email attachments, user and access management, automation and content policies, and a full report.

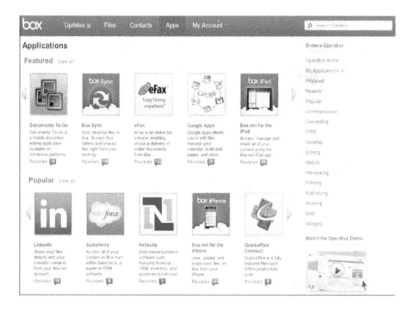

4.9 Waze

Waze is a system that uses GPS technology information that is returned from different devices, including iPhone, Android, Windows Mobile and Symbian. The initial version of this application was introduced in 2006. Waze implies a powerful ability to integrate with Twitter because people tweet about what is happening in their environment. You can report updated information on traffic accidents and police sightings. Waze is different with traditional GPS navigation software in which it is designed as community driven and collects complementary map data with traffic information from its users. People can report certain urban information, such as accidents, traffic jams, and police traps. Although Waze can be used worldwide, it is up to a critical mass of users to have real utility. It contains amazing features that make this application attractive to any controller. This application guides drivers, syncs calendar events, creates route plans, gets gas, and watches over friends.

4.10 CloudApp

The largest category of cloud-based consumer applications is recoverable storage. This category can be easily understood because it is a service that anyone needs to have. CloudApp is a consumer app for Mac OS and iOS right now. The main innovation of this application is that it is creating a small ecosystem around it. CloudApp uses your selection of quick and easy body movements to designate a file or object to stream to cloud-based storage.

It includes a CloudApp icon on the taskbar that makes dragging and dropping the object easier. This application greatly improves which object can be easily loaded and how such objects can be used in their native context. The screenshot is an obvious example for such operations in a way that you can specify a key to take a screenshot to load in one go. When the recipient shows your link, they click on the link to see your screen. CloudApp includes some features, such as easy to use, easy to understand, share files and links, upload via drag and drop or global keyboard shortcuts, share drops using private or public links, view a history of your drops directly from the menu , re-copy links to a drop, change the privacy level of a drop, remove drops from the menu, rename drops from the menu and personalized upload notifications.

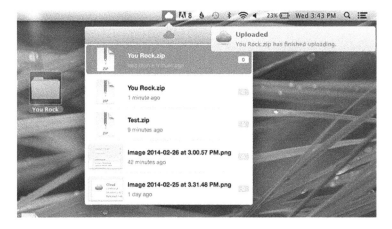

5 THE USES OF CLOUD SYSTEMS IN REAL-WORLD DOMAINS

Today, many institutes use cloud-based systems, either directly (e.g., Google and Amazon) or indirectly (e.g., Twitter), instead of using traditional on-site alternatives. Because cloud computing has more potential benefits, it is widely used by a large number of organizations. The uses of cloud systems have been a growth in the last decade. This section explains the uses of cloud computing in education, monitoring, healthcare, library, and banking.

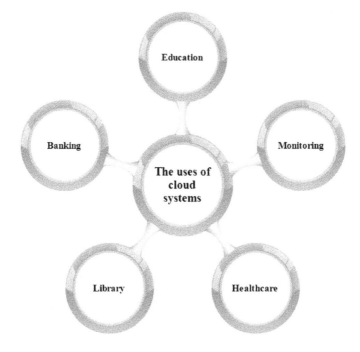

5.1 Education with cloud computing

IT professionals in educational institutions need to respond quickly to the different demands of teachers and students. In this area, cloud-based systems have become potential tools for delivering educational services in a more secure, reliable, and cost-effective manner. Education with cloud computing has some benefits, such as remodeling teaching through the extension of interactive multimedia tools, speeding up the delivery of administrative services, simplifying the required educational operations, saving process time, reducing financial costs, and reducing risks and strengthen security.

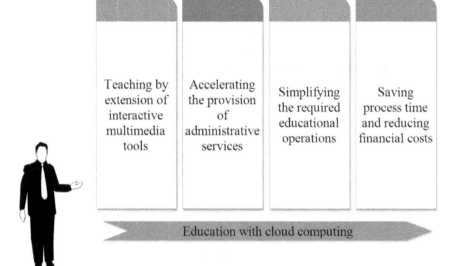

5.1.1 Cloud computing for the learning process

Educational organizations around the world depend on IT systems to supply their business requirements. Acquiring and maintaining a wide range of hardware and software require considerable investment and technical skills to support IT systems. The important features of cloud computing (e.g., scalability) are some reasons to increase the distance from traditional hosted services. Cloud-based services are progressively provided to people using Internet technology so that they can be easily accessed from web browsers (e.g., Internet Explorer). They are supplied cheaply or free of charge to various educational institutes with high availability. Today, many educations have moved to cloud-based systems by getting their students' email address. Email is a basic standard service that can be easily used by third parties and is not essential for educational services. Microsoft and Google provide email services free of charge to educational institutions in many countries. They offer email as a small part of the larger application suites that are generally available to students. Microsoft Live@edu and Google for Education include some additional communication tools such as instant messaging along with other services, contact management and calendar software. In addition, there are official applications to create the different documents, such as documents processed by text, spreadsheets and presentations in these educational tools. Students can use the cloud-based storage space to save their produced documents in all kinds.

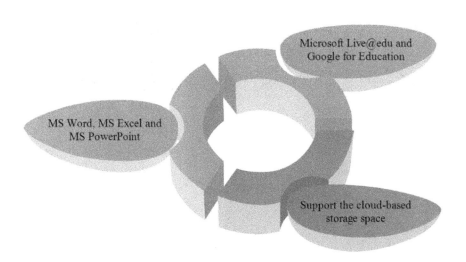

5.1.2 Free cloud tools available for education

Cloud services are provided free of charge to educational institutions. There are some significant benefits for companies that are currently competing for market share. The software has often been offered cheaply for education and vendors search to build relationships with the institutions they offer to their future employees. Furthermore, they are creating brand awareness and loyalty that may cause other premium services or services to be sold to institutions and clients in the future. A student who follows the advantages of such cloud-based tools can convince a future employer to be an investor in the commercial equivalents. Additionally, educational organizations have some IT plans to use low-level cloud-based services for different requirements (e.g., data storage). This capability will be more attractive when organizations need some of the open educational resources (e.g., video and audio). Another use of cloud-based systems in educational organizations is for the accommodation of Learning Management System (LMS). It will be used by organizations that cannot cover the costs of purchasing, maintaining and supporting software and hardware.

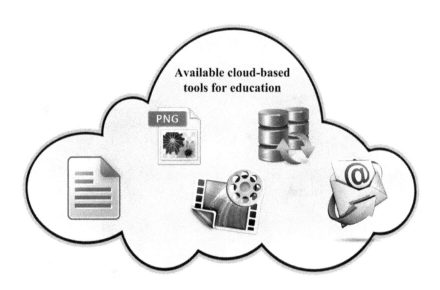

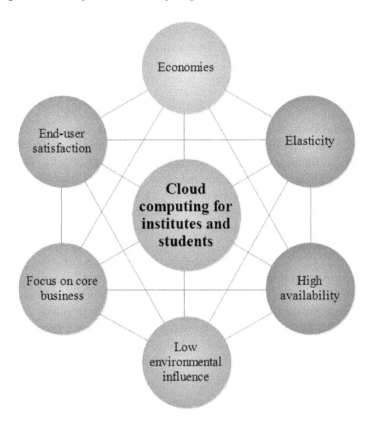

5.1.3 Benefits of cloud computing for institutes and students

It is obvious that cloud services have some potential benefits for educational institutions. These benefits are involved for the institutes themselves, students and teachers. This section explains some of these main benefits as follows.

Economies: The main benefit for many educational institutions is economic. This is especially obvious when some services (e.g., email) are provided free of charge by external providers. The hardware required for such services can be redeployed or removed in most cases. They can potentially be released for valuable real estate (e.g., college campuses in the city center) when a premium version is satisfied in the configuration. Meanwhile, some of the personnel costs can be greatly reduced. It is attractive now that educational institutions pay for use instead of often underused hardware.

Elasticity: Another advantage of cloud systems for education is the elastic capacity of these systems. It enables educational institutions to primarily start with small-scale cloud-based services and build moderately without any significant up-front investment. In addition, it enables rapid progress on demands at special times (e.g., at the beginning of the academic year or during exam periods). Therefore, it is not necessary to plan usage levels in the advanced state.

High availability: An additional advantage of cloud services in education is that availability is high with less downtime. The reason is that a cloud service provider accesses some superior resources and skills. Because a university's IT services department can focus on obtaining 99.5% availability for its educational services (e.g., LMS), Google provides 99.9% availability for the suite of educational applications. Students require online services for learning and assessment that must be obtained with the best possible availability.

Low environmental influence: Today, there are "green" targets to reduce energy consumption by organizations in some countries. Cloud servers allow educational organizations to minimize their own electricity consumption. Therefore, cloud service providers must optimize energy usage across a group of customers. Note that it is a bit difficult to get figures on the energy use of cloud providers, as well as their energy consumption worldwide is growing considerably.

Focus on core business: Another enhanced benefit of cloud computing for education is that it enables educational organizations to focus on their core research and education business. Universities and schools do not usually have their own power plants and excrement plants. Similarly, it can be argued that cloud-based computing services are improving to be commercialized and are being better manipulated by cloud institutions with particular skills and economies of scale.

End-user satisfaction: There are some obvious potential benefits to end users of cloud services, in addition to better availability, especially notable with the range of new applications on offer. Such benefits include the latest cloud application features and tools from innovative companies like Microsoft and Google. Based on these capabilities, teachers and students can freely use official applications without the need to purchase, install, and keep those applications up-to-date on their computers. Collaboration programs are greatly improved in this field. When data is secure and freely stored in a cloud-based space with large storage capacity, educational institutions do not worry about backing up or losing their data. Meanwhile, their data is available to them from any location around the world or from any device (e.g., mobile phone). Some advanced technologies (e.g.,

HTML5) will gradually allow users to work offline when there is no Internet access.

5.2 Cloud monitoring

Cloud monitoring is an extremely important task for both consumers and providers. It is a main tool for managing and controlling infrastructures in both aspects of hardware and software. In addition, it offers essential information and key performance indicators (KPIs) for applications and platforms. Both providers and consumers receive continuous monitoring in the cloud in different terms of availability, scalability and delay. It is done using some information, such as the workload generated by the later version and the performance and QoS provided by the cloud. In addition, some mechanisms necessary to recover and prevent violations for both the provider and the consumer to allow them in cloud-based monitoring systems.

5.2.1 Cloud monitoring basics

As indicated above, cloud monitoring is required to constantly evaluate the behaviors and infrastructures of the application in different terms of reliability, efficiency, energy use, security, etc. It is performed to conduct business analytics to improve application and system operations and for other occupations. This subsection introduces some fundamental concepts about cloud monitoring, which is used to discuss cloud computing for monitoring tasks.

5.2.1.1 Layers

Based on the work of the Cloud Security Alliance, a cloud system is modeled on seven layers, including facility, network, hardware, operating system, middleware, application, and user. These layers can be managed and controlled by a provider or a consumer. A brief description of each layer is detailed below.

At the facility layer, the physical infrastructure to create the data centers is considered to determine computing and network equipment. At the network layer, network links and routes for both the cloud and between the cloud and the user are considered. The physical components of computer and network equipment are considered at the hardware layer. At the operating system layer, software components are considered to build the operating system on both the host and user sides. Note that the host-side operating system runs on the physical machine and the user-side operating system runs on the virtual machine. At the middleware layer, the software layer between the operating system and user applications is carefully considered. Note that it is generally used only in cloud systems that offer SaaS and PaaS service models. The application run by the user of the cloud system is considered at the application layer. The user layer involves the end user of the cloud system and applications that run outside of the cloud server.

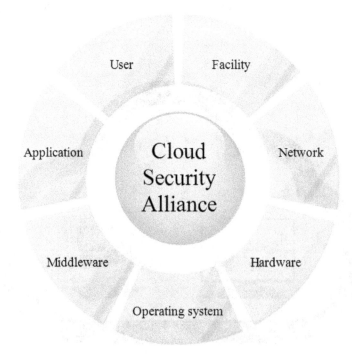

In cloud monitoring, these layers are considered to express the monitoring system probes. The layers have direct results, where the probes are located, in the phenomena observed by monitoring the cloud. Meanwhile, what era can be monitored inside and what era can be monitored outside of a cloud system are defined accordingly. Because the complexity of cloud systems is very high, it is not possible to investigate whether phenomena are literally monitored or not. This research concerns the cloud service provider who knows whether two applications are running on the same physical host or not. These problems increase when analyzing the efficiency of computing in terms of the time required to complete a task and the workload obtained by virtualized environments.

5.2.1.2 Abstraction levels

Cloud computing can implement low and high level monitoring. Low-level monitoring refers to information collected by cloud providers. It is often not disclosed to the consumer and is more related to the state of the physical infrastructure (e.g., the cloud server and storage media). In contrast, high-level monitoring refers to information about the state of the virtual platform. Cloud providers or consumers collect this information at the middleware, application, and user layers. This process is carried out through platforms and services controlled by themselves or by third parties. In the IaaS context, both levels are interested for both providers and consumers. In the SaaS context, high-level monitoring for consumers is more interesting and attractive than for providers. In low-level monitoring, special tools collect information at the hardware layer (e.g., CPU, memory, voltage, and workload), at the operating system layer, at the middleware layer (e.g., vulnerabilities in bug and software), at the network layer (e.g., general infrastructure security through firewall, IDS and IPS) and at the facility layer (e.g., physical security of completed facilities by observing rooms of the data center through authentication and video surveillance systems).

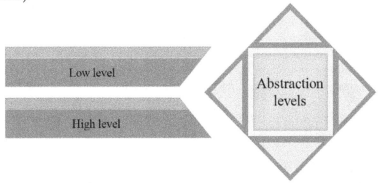

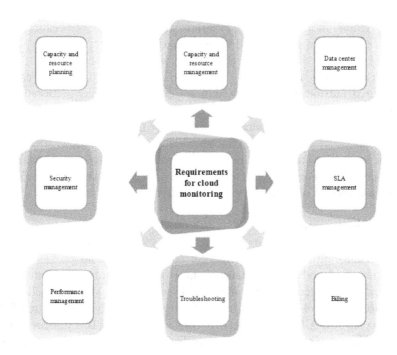

5.2.2 Requirements for cloud monitoring

Monitoring is obviously influential for all the key activities covered by cloud auditor. In a special view, cloud computing includes many activities to perform the essential tasks required for monitoring. This subsection carefully and accurately evaluates such activities through a procedure that underlines the role of monitoring for each of the activities. These activities are explained through a classification of the main aspects as follows.

Capacity and resource planning: This item is one of the most recommended tasks for service and application developers, before large-scale consideration of cloud computing. Due to the guarantee of efficiency required by services and applications, developers must measure the amount of capacity and resources to be purchased and must specify the anticipated workload. Note that capacity and resources depend on how these services and applications are designed and implemented by service providers. Actual values are unpredictable and highly variable because a prediction can be obtained through static analysis, testing, and monitoring operations. Cloud providers often offer guarantees in terms of QoS, capacity, and resources for their cloud-based services as determined in the SLA. They offer such guarantees because the developers of services and applications do not have any problem in this regard. Cloud-based service providers require cloud monitoring to anticipate and track the evolution of all parameters included in the QoS of cloud servers. This operation means that the infrastructure and resources to consider the SLA are carefully planned.

Capacity and resource management: A monitoring system with the ability to accurately capture is required to manage and control a complex and sophisticated system similar to a cloud system. The virtualization process has become a major component in designing and implementing cloud systems in recent years. By hiding the heterogeneous high resources of physical infrastructure and platforms, virtualization technology presents another sophisticated level for infrastructure providers. It leads to managing and controlling physical and virtualized resources. Meanwhile, it makes virtualized resources to migrate easily and quickly from one physical machine to another at any time. Therefore, the monitoring process is essential in cloud-based scenarios to manage resource volatility and rapidly change network situations. The use of IaaS to obtain QoS and quality of protection (QoP) is very necessary in critical public services (e.g., healthcare applications). Especially, organizations and customers consider such services to have 100% uptime when using cloud based infrastructures. Therefore, flexible and reliable monitoring of the entire cloud infrastructure is needed to offer availability to companies and people.

Data center management: Cloud-based services and systems are provided by large-scale data centers, where the management is an essential task. This task is literally a key part of resource management and an importance of your weird requirements. Data center management activities (e.g., data center control) use two fundamental tasks that include monitoring and data analysis. The monitoring activity tracks the required hardware and software metrics. In contrast, data analysis uses such metrics to shut down application and system states for resource provisioning, troubleshooting, and other administration tasks. Both monitoring and data analysis activities should support real-time operations to manage these data centers carefully and appropriately. They must scale proportionally to tens of thousands of heterogeneous stations to handle sophisticated I/O structures and network topologies. Keep in mind that network energy efficiency is a key requirement for data monitoring and analysis to achieve resource planning, sourcing, and management.

SLA management: Cloud computing provides the unprecedented flexibility for resource management to define new programming models. This process leads to cloud applications taking some advantages that arise from these new monitoring functions. It is mandatory and instrumental that compliance with the SLA is certified by the monitoring capacity in a way that the activities are used to consider the regulation (e.g., involving government data and services). Ultimately, cloud monitoring enables providers to use knowledge of user-recognized efficiency to formulate realistic and dynamic SLAs and to improve realistic pricing models.

Billing: This feature is an essential feature for measuring the services that cloud computing should offer. Billing allows the consumer to pay proportionally for the use of cloud-based services with various metrics and different granularity. The billing process is carried out according to the type of service and the price model. Contemporary customer numbers, total customer base, and application-specific performance levels are a few examples of billing criteria for SaaS. Furthermore, CPU utilization and task completion time are two examples for PaaS, as well as the number of VMs and possibly the variation with different CPU/memory installations are two examples for IaaS. Monitoring is essential on both the provider side for billing and the consumer side to verify its own use for each of the service models and pricing models. It can also be used to compare different providers with each other.

Troubleshooting: The complex and sophisticated infrastructure of a cloud system illustrates major challenges to solving problems (e.g., root cause analysis). These challenges cause a major problem with finding multiple possible components (e.g., network and host) that build multiple layers (e.g., virtual hardware, host, and guest OS). Therefore, providers must have a comprehensive, reliable, and scheduled monitoring framework to locate the problem within their sophisticated infrastructure and to alarm consumers to realize that any problems or performance failures are occurring.

Performance management: The cloud computing model has become very attractive to most consumers, especially midsize companies and research groups, because it offers the maintenance of hardware infrastructure to cloud providers. However, it is possible that the performance obtained by some cloud nodes is worse than that obtained by other cloud nodes. Variability and availability of efficiency are very important and critical when a consumer uses a public cloud to host a mission critical service or to work with scientific applications. Therefore, the performance of a monitoring platform is very necessary from the consumer's perspective to adjust changes or take corrective measures. For example, a consumer may like to host the required applications in multiple clouds to ensure high availability and to switch between different clouds based on measured performance. Regarding the contents represented above, monitoring is very essential to improve the efficiency of real applications and affect activity planning and repeatability of experiments.

Security management: Several important reasons make cloud security very important and critical. Security is one of the most notable barriers to spreading cloud computing and considering undeniable types of applications (e.g., a business-critical application) and consumers (e.g., a government). There are different works that offer some recommendations for reviews and security in the cloud. Some appropriate monitoring systems are needed to manage and control security in cloud-based infrastructure and services. In addition, clouds should improve strict regulations to host critical services for public uses. It may be available using a potential monitoring system that enables the evaluation process to certify compliance with regulations and to maintain a customer's data within the country's borders.

5.3 Healthcare

Health centers must offer new and better care operations to their patients. In addition, they should limit any increase in healthcare costs. Cloud computing as an advanced IT toolkit can play an important role in the healthcare and patient areas to improve healthcare operations under various ordinary or urgent conditions. It has some important and potential benefits for improving the healthcare process through technology. Note that there are some important challenges and barriers such as security, privacy, reliability, integration, and data portability in this field to implement drug applications by could-based systems.

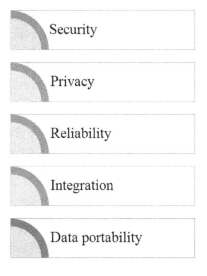

Security

Privacy

Reliability

Integration

Data portability

5.3.1 Data portability

Data portability is a capability that effects on willingness of some healthcare organizations to use cloud computing in the related areas. It is used to transfer data from a cloud vendor to another vender and to come back to the healthcare organization without having any disrupting operations or conflicted data. Healthcare organizations could physically control and manage their systems, services, and data by traditional IT systems. In such systems, when a cloud provider suspends its services or denies access to data, the healthcare organization cannot suddenly access its service and patient information. Furthermore, the process of migrating from the current cloud provider to another provider will be very challenging when the healthcare organization notices that the cloud service is suddenly suspended. Therefore, it indicates that the provider agreement is very essential and leads to address termination rights, data access rights anywhere, rights to retrieve data at any time and have a wizard for migration to another service provider.

5.3.2 Capabilities of cloud-based healthcare applications

One of the key trends in the use of healthcare is patient centrality. It leads to constant growth in selecting electronic health records, personal health records, electronic medical records, integrated care, clinical information, and clinical decision support. Patient satisfaction and high-priced clinical outcomes can be achieved through data availability and regardless of patient and physician location. Cloud computing can greatly facilitate these trends. Cloud-based systems bring potential benefits to healthcare applications, such as physician clinics, hospitals, and health clinics. Such applications should involve quick and easy access to large computing and storage capabilities that are not available in traditional IT systems. Because healthcare providers and patients can use healthcare data to prevent significant delay in treatment and waste of time, they need to be shared across multiple settings and geographies. Cloud-based servers provide these requirements to healthcare organizations as an incredible opportunity to improve the different services offered to their clients and patients, share healthcare data across multiple healthcare branches, and improve the performance of health operations.

Some capabilities of cloud computing for healthcare applications are explained below. Clinical research is one of the important capabilities that cloud systems can achieve. A large number of pharmacology providers enhance their research and drug developments through cloud computing. The excessive effectiveness of biological products in the research process is an instance of this development. It is usually done due to decreased cost and improved development performance of new drugs. Electronic medical record is another capability that cloud systems can design and facilitate. It leads doctors and hospitals to view cloud-based medical information and medical image files. Furthermore, this feature makes clinical support systems considerably better. Cloud computing-based medical collaboration solutions are another capability that can be used for rural telehealth or disaster response. They can be implemented through a mobile environment with wide wireless broadband and smartphone adoption. Cloud technology applies the use of collaboration and team healthcare to meet the requirements of the business model and public set of clinical information. Telemedicine is another capability in this area to conduct teleconsultation and telesurgery and to provide health record exchange, video conferencing, and home monitoring. Healthcare organizations can use cloud computing to locally reduce hardware storage costs. They can store big data for some requirements, like drug information, radiology imaging, and genomic data. In fact, cloud-based systems are used to facilitate healthcare data breaches compared to traditional client-server systems.

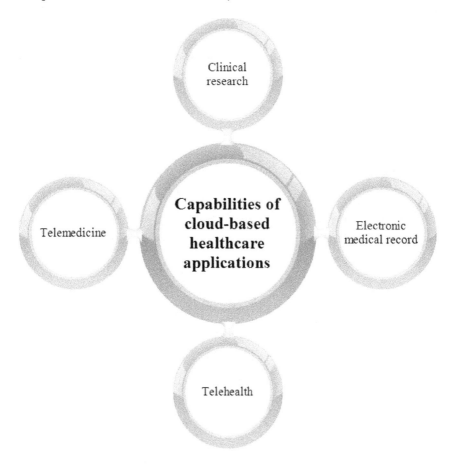

5.4 Libraries

Cloud-based servers can develop and extend libraries to store various book data and facilitate customer interactions. They use cloud computing concepts to empower the effectiveness of cooperation and to build a meaningful and unified presence in the web environment. These processes lead to saving time and money and increasing customer satisfaction. Cloud organizations need to consider some limited conditions to apply potential cloud computing enhancements to libraries. Some of these conditions are listed as follows. Most of the existing computer systems in libraries are based on pre-web technology. Systems built over the network using pre-web technology are more difficult and expensive to integrate easily. Much of the same data are stored and maintained hundreds and thousands of times. Collaborating libraries with independent systems is difficult and expensive. Information seekers have some challenges getting the library into their workflow because they work with prevalent web environments and distributed systems, and many systems only use 10% of their capacity. Finally, they can be classified into three groups that include technology, data and community. Note that each of them offers some general and some unique opportunities for libraries. The use of cloud computing in libraries can be explained through four elements, including technology improvement, data efficiency, community efficiency, and discovery service.

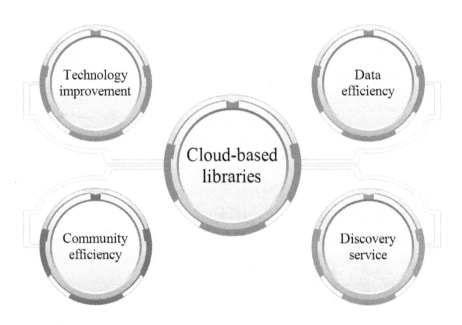

5.4.1 Technology improvement

Cloud computing for libraries is planned based on current technology, because it is designed to allow for technological changes. A look at the use of mobile devices in companies and organizations through a cloud environment indicates that new technologies are capable, quickly and economically, to reorganize and deliver services to their customers through new devices. Before researchers introduced the Internet and the web, library management systems were provided for libraries to do the required tasks. These systems have some challenges to use the potential benefits of new technologies. In the meantime, they should integrate external systems and libraries through their providers to present new developments for the libraries. In addition, libraries must add additional systems to control their changeable collections in a way that physical collection management is strictly transformed into a combination of digital, physical and licensed collections. Integration of these systems is often impossible and difficult because the systems have stood alone. Libraries can present innovative services to their clients through cloud-based servers. Their existing services can be redeployed to expand to cloud-based services in the environment.

5.4.2 Data efficiency

Maintaining and storing data on cloud servers offer libraries several advantages. Sharing common data between services and customers is one of these advantages. There is no need for local storage, maintenance and backup operation. The data can be provided privately to a special organization and company. Finally, libraries are able to scale the web due to the huge amount of data and clients. Like the benefits of cloud-based technologies to solve existing problems in various areas, cloud-based storage achieves potential benefits for libraries. Bulk data can be stored and maintained hundreds and thousands of times in libraries by cloud servers. When multiple copies of the cataloging data are available for a serial publication like The Economist, they can be kept on cloud-based servers to make them readily available to many libraries, to be carefully changed by supported institutions, and to be backed up more quickly times. Web presence will be difficult for libraries if library data is widely disseminated on many systems. Because search engines (e.g., Google, Yahoo, and Bing) can access library data, the search engine must be carefully optimized. Moreover, library collections should appear more relevant to search engines because they are displayed higher in search results.

5.4.3 Community efficiency

Libraries can create an online community information network with the unique opportunity based on cloud computing. They offer internal and external communities to collaborate within a single institution and across multiple institutions. Cooperative library efforts can create some of the essential savings and efficiencies at scale to deliver collaborative intelligence for better decision making and innovative platforms. Both companies and organizations create social communities around the world using the external community to present their services to customers. In addition, the internal community offers new possibilities and efficiencies for today's library workflows. A large number of librarians have revealed the potential benefits of cloud-based services (e.g., Google Docs) to jointly decrease the effectiveness of workloads. These services share ongoing programs anytime, anywhere. Libraries can collaborate revolutionally in a cloud environment. Some appropriate decisions regarding collection development, preservation, and digitization can be made if data and functions are shared in cloud-based libraries.

5.4.4 Discovery service

Libraries can get new performances from both the internal community and the library community. There is library software that creates internal and external characters to use the potential benefits of new technologies and web capabilities in the library community. It causes globally building a large network of librarians that is used to communicate between libraries and to answer specific questions. Changes in library collections occur between traditional job roles in libraries. Meanwhile, electronic material licenses must be managed, and the purchase of multiple formats must be carefully controlled. Therefore, a unified form is required in a way that information can be made available from providers, reviewers, local constituencies and other staff. These requirements are developed so that an open system accesses the information through external systems and obtains data and services from these systems. Cloud computing creates some new workflows that librarians require because it provides a significant opportunity for a cooperative platform between libraries. A cooperative platform has four main principles, including openness, extensibility, data richness, and collaboration. Openness means that data and services can be accessed through the library and third-party applications due to significant interoperability support within and between cloud services. Extensibility means that the platform, which is extended by the service provider or community members, can help the process of adding new services and applications. Data richness means that libraries can interact with large amounts of purchased, licensed, and digital information. Finally, collaboration means that a library can use the collective power of the library community to present new solutions.

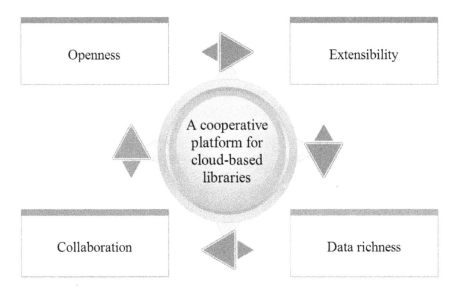

5.5 Banking

Banking and Financial Service (BFS) institutions use the most advanced features of new technologies and the potential capabilities of cloud computing to support their clients. Banking institutions use the potential capabilities of cloud-based servers that utilize high-level business automation, considerable progress in functional applications, and the benefits of outsourcing processing technology. That is, the performance of financial institutions can be improved by cloud computing in several significant ways. The use of cloud computing in banking systems can be provided through four terms, including cost savings, business continuity, business agility, and green IT. These terms are briefly explained as follows.

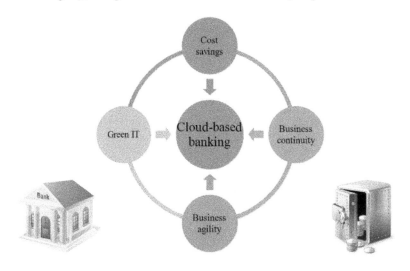

Cloud computing can provide significant features to financial institutions because it saves huge operating costs. These institutions reduce large amounts of previous costs into smaller and more continuous operating costs. There is no need to invest large costs to buy new hardware and software. In addition, cloud-based systems allow financial institutions to serve their clients on a pay-as-you-go basis. Business continuity means that the service provider manages the technology through cloud computing. Financial institutions gain a higher level of fault tolerance, disaster recovery, and data protection. Keep in mind that the redundancy and backup prices offered by cloud systems are lower than those offered by traditional managed solutions. The potential features of cloud-based systems allow financial institutions to use short development cycles for new products. This means that the needs of bank customers are answered more quickly and efficiently. Because cloud systems are used as required, fewer infrastructure investments are required so that initial implementation costs are saved considerably. No capital investment is needed to develop new products. Note that cloud computing allows companies to remove some common services, such as software patches and maintenance. Green IT in banking systems means that banking institutions use cloud computing to transfer their services to a virtual environment. It causes lower energy consumption and carbon footprint. Furthermore, it improves the efficiency of cloud capabilities and reduces downtime.

6 THE SECURITY ISSUES OF CLOUD SERVERS

Previously, cloud computing was a promising business concept. Today, it is promoted to one of the fastest growing parts of the IT industry. A lot of diverse organizations realize that they can gain rapid access to business applications and increase infrastructure resources through cloud-based systems. Because large amounts of information from individuals and organizations are stored and maintained on cloud servers, cloud providers must carefully ensure the security of systems. The security issues of cloud servers are classified into several elements, including security, privacy, reliability, legal issues, open standard, compliance, freedom, long-term viability, and data ownership.

6.1 Security

In some situations, the data stored on local hard drives is safe, and in some other situations, the data stored on high security servers is safe. Some claims indicate that customer data managed at local warehouses is more secure, and others claim that cloud service providers employ a higher level of security. Since your data will be stored and distributed on multiple individual computers, the data security will be considerably high. The locations of these computers do not depend on where your data warehouse is ultimately stored. Because professional hackers can invade virtually any cloud-based server, storing data on multiple servers can be very secure. Since there is no public cloud security standard, there are additional challenges associated with this issue. Many cloud service providers design and implement their own proprietary standards and security technologies to use different security models that must be analyzed and evaluated on their own servers.

6.2 Privacy

Privacy is an important area in cloud computing. It is difficult to satisfy even with traditional security systems and networks. Cloud computing has considerable and key suggestions for document and file privacy. Meanwhile, it guarantees the confidentiality characteristic of commercial and government information. The existing privacy suggested by today's cloud systems is obvious and real. Because critical and essential information for individual and business uses are placed on a third-party cloud service provider in public clouds, this concern is true and valid on these types of cloud servers. Such situations occur when the cloud infrastructure cannot be regulated and can be traversed across geographic boundaries. Information on cloud servers are recognized as having fragile privacy characteristics over personal computer systems. Therefore, users of cloud servers should know the main terms of the contract they sign with a cloud service provider. In addition, they must obtain primary information about privacy and security guidelines from cloud service providers. To achieve such information, the different privacy and security requirements of cloud models must be carefully investigated and controlled. The reason is that the privacy and confidentiality issues of all cloud models are not the same with each other. That is, any cloud model provides special security requirements, privacy capabilities, and various cost implications. Although private clouds are more expensive to operate in cloud environments, they are more appropriate for protected materials and classified information. Moreover, public clouds are more appropriate for personal and non-confidential information.

6.3 Reliability

The servers used by cloud systems involve the same problems that occurred on their own resident servers. Moreover, cloud servers can have downtime and slowdowns in some situations. Therefore, users in the cloud computing model have a greater dependence on the cloud service provider (CSP). When a user selects a particular CSP, the service model will be different so that the user can be locked up and a potential commercial security risk will be introduced to the server. Reliability in cloud servers can be classified into four groups: maximize service availability for users, minimize the impact of any failure on users, maximize service efficiency, and maximize business continuity. Maximizing service availability means that cloud servers do whatever users want for most of the time possible. Minimizing the impact of any failure means that the service does not include non-critical components when something goes wrong. Maximizing service efficiency means that the impact to users will be reduced when efficiency is adversely affected (e.g., during an unexpected spike in traffic). Finally, maximizing business continuity means that the organization and service must respond carefully to users when a failure occurs.

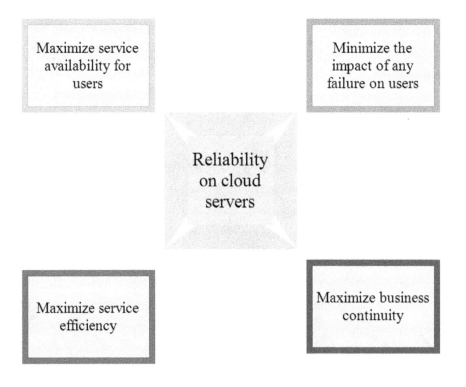

6.4 Legal issues

Legal and regulatory issues applied to cloud computing are dynamic. There are new laws to change the responsibilities of cloud service providers. Cloud computing creates dynamic new conditions in the relationship between an institution and information in the presence of a cloud provider. It creates some challenges to use the laws in a wide area of information management systems. Regardless of the cloud model used by the cloud system, legal issues must be considered in the area that collects, stores, and processes institution-related data. There are three types of laws, including state, national and international, that must be considered to ensure compliance with the law. Some of these laws are used in some special markets, such as the Health Insurance Portability and Accountability Act (HIPAA) for healthcare applications. Laws and regulations often determine who within a business environment should be responsible for ensuring the accuracy and security of data. If you collect and store data on cloud-based storage, you must have a designated security location to ensure legal compliance. If you use a cloud infrastructure offered by a cloud provider, you should be aware of all legal and regulatory requirements that apply to your business at the provider. In addition, there are some key issues to consider at all stages of the contractual process, including initial due diligence, contract negotiation, implementation, termination, and supplier transfer.

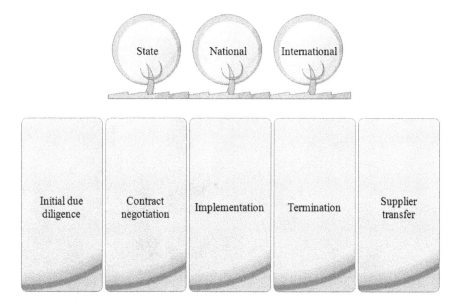

6.5 Open standard

The open standard is one of the essential tools to progress in cloud computing. Most cloud service providers reveal APIs that generally register well and refer exclusively to the implementation phase. Some cloud providers use the APIs of other service providers so that the cloud system develops a series of open standards. Most major companies (e.g., IBM) have come together to establish open standards based on cloud servers. One of their important goals is to promote open source technologies and open standards for cloud computing. Any company offering cloud services should focus on the wide adoption of open source platforms and open standards. This adoption means that customers have no fear of vendor blocking and institutions provide a wide area of cloud servers and cloud service providers. Various industries (e.g., healthcare and financial services applications) can share information quickly and easily at lower leading costs with open standards. They will be able to share innovative ideas in a spectacular and fast way. Open standards will accelerate technology adoption and technology values delivered by cloud-based customers. Besides, they have some potential benefits, such as establishing and adopting cloud paradigms for end users, reducing barriers to different inputs (e.g., development skills and freedom of choice) in cloud computing, increasing the long-term viability of investments in the cloud, and preventing unnecessary architectural complexity and fragmentation.

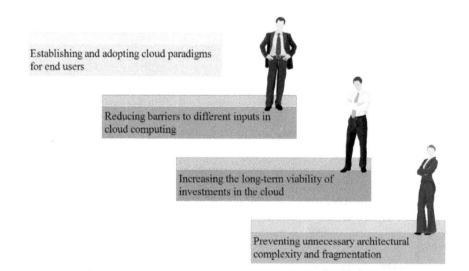

Establishing and adopting cloud paradigms for end users

Reducing barriers to different inputs in cloud computing

Increasing the long-term viability of investments in the cloud

Preventing unnecessary architectural complexity and fragmentation

6.6 Compliance

Cloud service providers must enable their clients to adequately comply with numerous regulations, such as regular reports and audit trails. An overview of IT resources can be achieved within a cloud-based location to deliver robust management and enforcement of compliance policies through compliance management and security for cloud computing. Customers and data centers maintained by cloud service providers are subject to compliance requirements. Any rule requires organizations to adequately protect their physical and information resources through some virtual ways. To achieve this purpose, some important requirements are suggested, such as the type of information stored and maintained in a system, the location of the storage media, a list of customer accounts that access the system, the information and the documents that can be accessed by customers and authentication of access to information. All of these requirements refer to the level of ownership of assets that indicate where cloud compliance issues become obvious. Cloud compliance changes the landscape for public cloud providers. Public service providers will need to be compliant with standards and should include contractual language to help customers meet cloud compliance requirements.

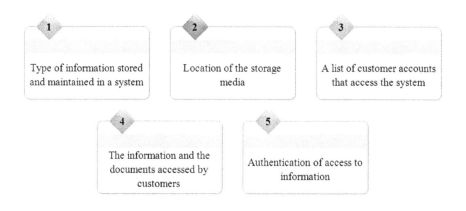

6.7 Freedom

Cloud servers do not allow users to physically own the data storage. These storages can be controlled and managed by cloud service providers. Clients will agree on some significant fundamental conditions applied at these providers. In addition, they may retain their own copies of data so that their freedom of choice is well preserved and protected against certain problems beyond their control. Those of the organizations that use cloud servers in different work areas, provide a series of freedom solutions through some specific modules. Freedom access platforms on cloud systems are focused on ensuring that all customers have all essential resources at hand. Customers can use this capability over the Internet remotely. Freedom access to cloud servers adds multiple services into one easy-to-use portal so customers can come back again and again. All the services integrated into the free access platforms allow your establishment to use the cloud capabilities carefully and easily. They are completely flexible and cheap in terms of use every month. Moreover, they are able to adapt to your needs in a way that you will not end up buying the extra services more than you need. All the capabilities mentioned above will improve and enhance your services. They provide a collaborative platform to improve service performance of cloud systems.

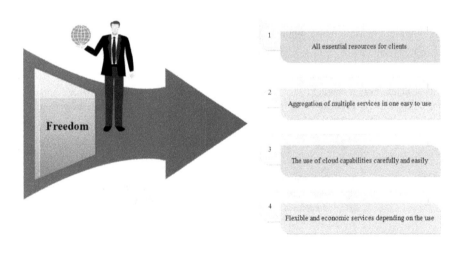

6.8 Long-term viability

Long-term viability in cloud computing means that a customer ensures that the data put into a cloud-based server will always be valid, even if the cloud service provider goes bankrupt. Cloud storage services are highly regarded by institutions because such services are widely adopted by customers and share some common features of other cloud services. They cause the emergence of infinite computing resources available on demand, the initial commitment is eliminated, and customers can purchase computing resources. In addition, the infrastructure of the cloud service can be owned, built and controlled by third parties. Because the technical realization of the public cloud is basically no different than the private cloud, various customer controls over data, security, and the network are carefully limited. Most cloud storage services use a business model, called Freemium. This model is characterized by freely granting a level of consumption to customers during which to earn money at the premium rate. Cloud storage service providers often offer basic features like file sharing, syncing, and a certain amount of free space. Because many customers expect basic features to be free, the Freemium business model has become very popular.

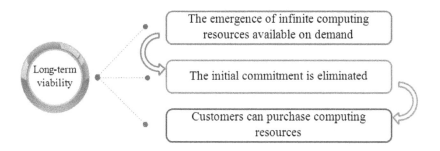

6.9 Data ownership

Ownership of the data and information residing in the cloud service provider is another issue to consider before the migration process to cloud computing. When a customer places data in cloud storage, data privacy can be lost not only, but also data ownership and the right of disclosure. Although legal ownership and right of disclosure reside with a special data owner, this process can change quickly. Some cloud service providers retain the right of disclosure as a data saver, while other service providers do not perform this process. This process changes moderately under the various terms of the contract that the cloud provider offers to its customers. There is an anxiety when the cloud service provider operates as a data owner and a data saver. Duties can be carefully separated even with traditional IT services where an individual service provider owns the data, while another individual service provider or a group of multiple service providers is the data saver. This cloud-related scheme means that a cloud service provider is both the owner of the data and the protector of all data or information that are stored and transmitted from cloud servers. It is suggested that cloud users protectively highlight their data and information, as well as explicitly determine the ownership of the data and information in the service contract. In addition, the service contract must be signed and approved by the cloud service provider in the form of a declaration.

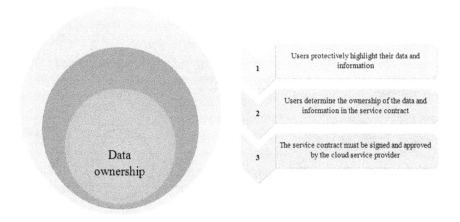

7 SIMULATION TOOLS FOR CLOUD APPLICATIONS

Cloud-based services can be run on cloud servers so that different results appear compared to the others. These servers may or may not be successful in executing the desired services. Before the implementation of the services on the real cloud servers, simulation platforms can be used to carry out the test phase. Any organization that provides cloud systems considers this process before the actual implementation of the cloud. It will lead to reducing the critical risks associated with actual implementation. There are several tools and simulation environments for cloud computing that are available to give practical phases of experience.

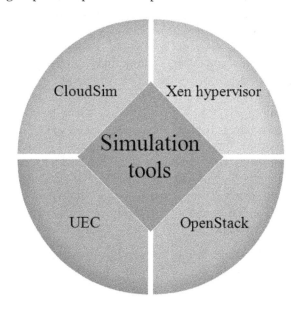

Cloud service providers will be able to deploy multiple cloud servers using these tools. Simulation tools for cloud computing are available with various features. Some of them implement public cloud environments and others implement private cloud environments. Any of them can be applied with respect to the choice of the experiment required for a special service. This section explains a comparison analysis for some of the simulation tools. For this purpose, several significant parameters are applied to perform the comparison process. Any cloud user can use these comparisons to choose an appropriate toolkit based on the needs and types of experiments.

7.1 CloudSim

CloudSim is an extensible simulation platform that enables the modeling and simulation processes of cloud systems and applications by provisioning cloud-based environments. This toolkit can support both systems and behaviors that model cloud-based system components (e.g., data centers, VMs, and policy resources). CloudSim is a framework for modeling and simulating cloud computing infrastructure and services. It has three potential benefits including effectiveness over time, flexibility, and applicability for initial performance tests. Time effectiveness means CloudSim requires very little workload and time to deploy cloud-based applications for test platforms. Flexibility and applicability mean that cloud service developers can model and test the efficiency of their applications across various cloud platforms (e.g., Microsoft Azure and Amazon EC2) using little code programming and implementation efforts.

The CloudSim software framework is comprised of a multi-layered design with various architectural components. The first layer is a simulation engine that supports several main functionalities, such as the processing of existing events, the creation of system entities in the cloud (e.g., data centers, intermediaries and VMs), communication between components and simulation clock management. The simulation layer models and simulates cloud-based virtualized data centers, including dedicated management interfaces for VMs, memory, cloud-based storage, and bandwidth. Meanwhile, it handles fundamental issues like provisioning the hosts available to VMs, managing application execution, and monitoring the dynamic state of the system. User code is the top layer of this platform that reveals the basic entities for hosts (e.g., number of machines and physical machine characteristics), applications (e.g., number of tasks and requirements tasks), VMs, number of users, types of user applications and broker scheduling policies.

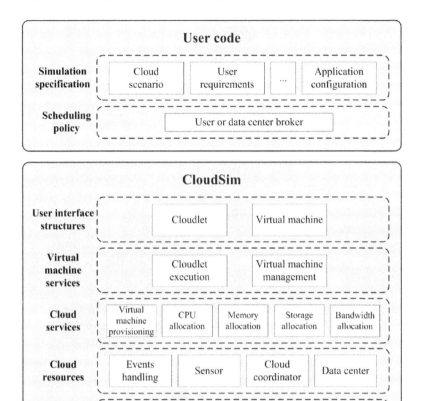

7.2 Xen hypervisor

The Xen hypervisor is a layer of software that runs directly on the computer hardware replacing the operating system. Thus, it allows the computer hardware to run multiple guest operating systems simultaneously. The Xen hypervisor supports various familiar platforms and operating systems to run on the hypervisor as a guest. Each computer running the Xen hypervisor includes three main components. It contains the configuration part and various components necessary to build the platform that runs on cloud servers. This platform runs directly on the computer hardware so that it becomes the main interface for hardware requests. It will be able to run multiple operating systems, safely and independently, isolating guests from computer hardware. The Domain & Guest, denoted by Dom0, is launched by the simulator at the initial system startup.

Domain & Guest	 Domain Guest	...	 Domain Guest

Xen hypervisor

Hardware

This simulator can be run on any operating system except Windows. Dom0 includes some unique access privileges that are not granted to other domain guests. The Domain Guest, indicated by DomUs, is launched and managed by Dom0 in a way that it operates on the computer system independently. The domain guests run with a specific modified operating system, called paravirtualization, or with unmodified operating systems that use specific virtualization hardware, called hardware virtual machine.

7.3 UEC

Ubuntu Enterprise Cloud (UEC) is a simulation platform for Canonical cloud computing involved with Ubuntu Server distribution. It contains Eucalyptus along with a large amount of open source software. UEC has a potential benefit to easily install and configure cloud systems. Additionally, Canonical offers some commercial technical support for the UEC toolkit. UEC is made up of various components including node controller, cloud controller, cluster controller, Walrus storage controller, and storage controller. The details of these components are explained below. The node controller is a UEC node that can run a kernel-based virtual machine (KVM) as a hypervisor. The UEC toolkit installs KVM automatically when the user wants to install the UEC node. VMs running on the hypervisor and managed by UEC are called instances. The node controller runs on any node and manages the life cycle of multiple instances running on the UEC node. This node interacts with the operating system and the hypervisor running on the node on one side and the cluster controller on the other side. Requests from the operating system running on the node locate the node's physical resources, such as the number of cores, memory size, and available disk space. Furthermore, it queries about the status of the VMs instances running on the node. The cluster controller controls one or more node controllers and deploys multiple instances to them. In addition, it manages the network function for multiple instances running on the nodes under given classifications of Eucalyptus network modes.

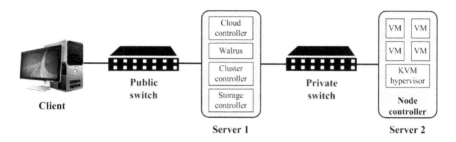

The cluster controller communicates with the cloud controller on one side and the node controller on the other side. The Walrus storage controller offers a simple persistent storage service by REST and SOAP compatible with APIs. It should be applied as a simple file storage system. The storage controller offers persistent block storage for use by multiple instances. The cloud controller is the front of the entire cloud infrastructure. It offers an EC2/S3 compliant web services interface to client components on one side and interacts with other components of the Eucalyptus infrastructure on the other side. Additionally, the cloud controller offers a web interface to cloud users to control the given aspects of the UEC infrastructure. It involves a comprehensive knowledge base on the availability and uses of cloud resources and the state of the cloud system.

7.4 OpenStack

The OpenStack toolkit is a collection of open source technology tools that offers a scalable open source cloud computing platform. Currently, it establishes two projects in question, including OpenStack computation and OpenStack object storage.

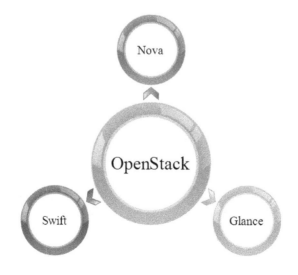

OpenStack computing provides computing power through VMs and the network management system. OpenStack object storage is an individual platform for redundant and scalable object storage capacity. The imaging service project, called Glance, is a platform closely related to the OpenStack computing project. This toolkit can be used by various companies, cloud service providers, researchers and global data centers. These capabilities can be enabled by deploying large-scale cloud deployment infrastructures for public or private clouds. The OpenStack platform includes three main families of services that include computing infrastructure (Nova), storage infrastructure (Swift) and imaging service (Glance).

8 CLOUD SERVICE PROVIDERS

There are a diverse number of companies that provide cloud services worldwide. Any one of them interacts with different clients, such as ordinary people, researchers and other organizations. They apply cloud capabilities to respond to their clients according to their requirements. Any business should offer cloud servers in a way that it increases the number of successful jobs, decreases the number of unsuccessful jobs, reduces response time, and greatly reduces the power consumption of cloud systems. This section explains some of the popular cloud providers that offer cloud environments for various models of cloud-based services.

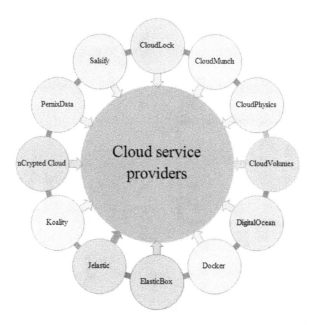

8.1 CloudLock

CloudLock provides security in addition to Google Apps and Salesforce by ensuring that critical and confidential information is carefully encrypted and saved. Gil Zimmermann is the founder and CEO of this company, who was a resident entrepreneur at Cedar Fund before co-founding CloudLock. Before that, he held a few positions at Sun and EMC corporations. Meanwhile, co-founder Tsahy Shapsa is formerly of Sun and Network Appliances. CloudLock was founded in 2007, but was renamed in 2010. Its investors are Cedar Fund, Ascent Venture Partners and Bessemer Venture Partners. Co-founders Shapsa and Zimmermann served in the Israeli Defense Forces and Shapsa was the leader of the security team in the office of the Israeli Prime Minister. Currently, both executives manage and control networking events in the Boston area for Israeli startups. Cloud computing fundamentally changes security models. It has potential, critical and confidential information about your cloud service provider instead of having it on your own premises beyond a firewall. CloudLock offers some convenient cloud models to protect the most critical and sensitive information. The company offers data security, encryption, and inspection services for workloads, particularly those in the clouds of Google and Salesforce. CloudLock creates some essential policies because it can identify all information and let customers know if the data is encrypted, where it is located, and who has access to it. It can search Google Drive and identify all credit cards and social security numbers that are kept in cloud stores to ensure they are properly encrypted. It applies cloud services APIs to protect systems, provide services, and run custom tools. CloudLock, itself, is hosted by Google Compute Engine and Amazon Web Services. It runs all the calculations, scans AES 256-bit encryption, and performs tasks without opening, reading, or storing any documents to ensure the security level of the clients.

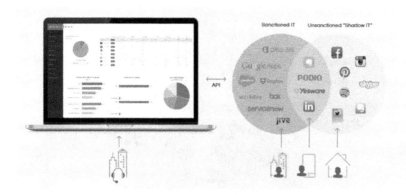

8.2 CloudMunch

CloudMunch provides the application lifecycle management software for DevOps and rapid development processes. Pradeep Prabhu is the founder and CEO of this company, who was vice president and chief of Infosys SaaS. Co-founder and CTO Prasanna Raghavendra was the engineering principle in Infosys SaaS. This company was founded in 2011 and Svapas Innovations is its investor. CloudMunch has a fully distributed staff around the world without a central office. All employees work remotely from their home locations, as well as company principles control and manage the operations required by their own technology. DevOps cooperatively systematizes the rules and ideas of software developers and infrastructure operations workers, but obtains them in readily available ways. CloudMunch has produced application life cycle management software because developers adopt an ingenious model for creating customer-facing, mobile, and web applications. CloudMunch works on a large number of infrastructure platforms or public and private clouds, from Amazon Web Services to Windows Azure and OpenStack. It is compatible with PaaS tools (e.g., Cloud Foundry and AWS Elastic Beanstalk). Developers can track and produce the application software in a collaborative process by having both developers and operators in the CloudMunch system. Additionally, they can report what cloud resources are required to run the application. Through this feature, infrastructure can be accessed from an application-centric point of view based on CloudMunch strategies. This company seeks to enter commercial markets, particularly those of companies that develop web, cloud, mobile, big data and customer-oriented applications.

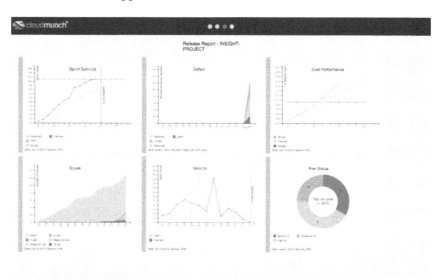

8.3 CloudPhysics

CloudPhysics applies a SaaS platform to offer big data analytics to optimize the ways in which data centers operate. John Blumenthal is the founder and CEO of this company, who was previously director of product management for VMware ESX storage stack and a Veritas Software worker. Meanwhile, CTO Irfan Ahmad was a VMware engineer, when Jim Klechner was with Currenex and chief scientist Xiaojun Liu engaged in Google, Salesforce and Sun. CloudPhysics was founded in 2011 by Kleiner Perkins Caufield & Byers, Mayfield Fund, Mark Leslie, Peter Wagner, Carl Waldspurger, Nigel Stokes, Matt Ocko, and three VMware co-founders, Diane Greene, Mendel Rosenblum, and Ed Bugnion. The company's CEO Blumenthal worked at VMware's market-leading ESX hypervisor for five years. Blumenthal and CloudPhysics use big data to answer complex and sophisticated questions about how systems exist and should run on servers. Clients download a virtual device that is connected to the virtual infrastructure by adding data from thousands of clients. By considering this wealth of information, CloudPhysics searches for paradigms of good and bad. The SaaS platform suggests some important settings for high performance, manages the basic analysis of problems that arise and helps professional operations determine the usefulness of a measure. A large number of companies offer resource optimization services for applications that take place in cloud environments. Virtualized environments have placed new resources on systems, creating a market opportunity for analysis of optimization operations.

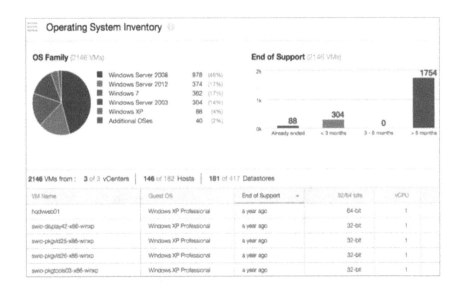

8.4 CloudVolumes

CloudVolumes is the application virtualization and management software. Raj Parekh is the founder and CEO of this company, who was the founder of Redwood Ventures and previously held CTO and vice president positions at Sun. Co-founder and CTO Matthew Conover was previously technical director at Symantec, when co-founder Shaun Coleman was director of product management for Citrix XenDesktop. The company was founded in 2011 by TiE Angels, Kumar Malavalli, Sanjog Gad, Rob Thomas, and Bill Crane who is formerly of vice president of engineering at LinkedIn and vice president of engineering at Proofpoint. CEO Parekh is a serial entrepreneur who founded Redwood Venture Partners in 1998. Note that Redwood Venture Partners has invested more than $250 million in thirty companies. CEO Parekh sits on the boards of more than fifteen companies. It is difficult for IT stores to compete with other companies in a world with so many applications. Employees, who use cloud applications without any IT knowledge, will face a huge logistical and security challenge. Businesses must obtain some ways to control or investigate these villain applications by allowing employees to produce a large number of applications. Such challenges arise under certain conditions into which CloudVolumes enters.

CloudVolumes software provides a way to control everything that is placed in an organization's operating system. The company necessarily virtualizes anything about the operating system, keeping applications away from hardware and networks. Once the app grows, you can have full control over it. In addition to the operating system application, the application will be allowed to be deployed on one or more machines, including having IT control over the application. Virtual desktops are one of the company's most popular tools.

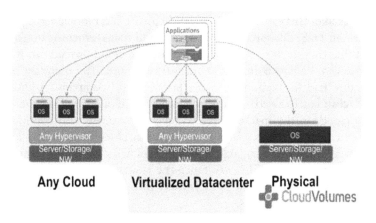

Any Cloud   **Virtualized Datacenter**   **Physical**
CloudVolumes

Once CloudVolumes is installed on the server, the software controls the critical database and application information required to run and create a volume with it. Therefore, this volume can be connected to one or more VMs. Applications may be available to one or more clients with a few clicks within an administration console. There is no company, except CloudVolumes, that virtualizes multiple layers of the stack from the compute, storage, and network layers. When you mount a remote server so that files and documents are accessible through a local file system, CloudVolumes will allow you to mount a complete stack of applications in which it is accessible on the local machine. This capability makes it easy to set up complete application stacks for desktops or servers. Any client can mount the desired application to make it available easily and quickly. Therefore, the client does not need to install or patch the application on every desktop or server computer, resulting in wasted time and error-proneness. CloudVolumes has entered into alliances with Citrix and Dell. Additionally, it makes the software available to run in VMware virtual environments.

8.5 DigitalOcean

DigitalOcean focuses on the deployment of public IaaS. The company's team came from the hosting company Server Stack. Ben Uretsky is the founder and CEO of this company, as well as Mitch Wainer is the marketing manager. DigitalOcean was founded in 2011 by Andreessen Horowitz, IA Ventures, CrunchFund, and TechStars. It has parted ways with the TechStars startup program, which offers seed funding with more than seventy-five venture capital firms and angel investors. This company is called DigitalOcean because it reveals some concepts for the computer services of the company, called Droplets. These concepts are similar to those formed by water in the ocean and create clouds. Some investors believe that the IaaS market has not been carefully considered. However, big players like Amazon Web Services, Microsoft and Google have put their purposes on IaaS. DigitalOcean's founders and management team focus on the fact that they want to run a managed hosting cloud provider so they can recognize one or two concepts about infrastructure. The company's cloud architecture had the same title in the IaaS GoGrid company. Additionally, DigitalOcean has focused on targeting expert developers and the most user-friendly cloud on the market. This company competes with confidence in service prices. It provides a base level virtual machine for less than a penny per hour ($0.007 per hour), although this level will only be performed with a minimum memory of 512 MB. Since the launch of DigitalOcean's cloud services to the general public is in January 2013, the company's customers have grown to 100,000 users.

8.6 Docker

Docker provides an alternative method to virtualization operations for application developers using containerization technology based on an open source project. dotCloud was founded in 2010 by Solomon Hykes as a PaaS company. Solomon and other members of the dotCloud management team launched Docker in March 2013. This project was an open source engine to establish any application and its dependency as a lightweight container, running virtually services anywhere in the world. The company changed its name to Docker in early 2013. Long distance trade has been used before the emergence of shipping containers which was much more difficult. Because the boxes and cargo had different shapes and sizes, they made the boats move with difficulty. Subsequently, Malcom McLean reorganized global trade in the 1950s using modern standardized metal containers to make it easier to grip the cranes. Everything can be filled inside a container to reach the final destination. The dubbed Linux containers are a proprietary version of shipping containers that can be filled with very attractive applications. They can run on various platforms, such as public clouds, virtualized private clouds, and simple non-virtualized servers. Docker is the corporation that helps market the open source version of the Docker project. It can be used to design, create, assemble and manage these computer containers more easily. This company changed its name from dotCloud to Docker due to the purchase of a new executive team and the signing of partnerships with Red Hat and OpenStack. If a customer does not need operating system heterogeneity, Docker system-level virtualization makes perfect sense.

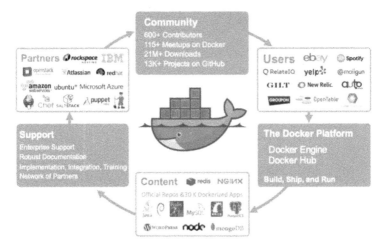

Containers allow four times as many instances in the operating system by creating a virtual version of the system level instead of the hardware level through a traditional hypervisor. Docker sponsors declare that containers can have potential benefits over VMs. All existing applications in containers must be running on the same operating system without having the ability to control the operating system. Please note that this weakness may not be a critical problem for a Windows or Linux store.

8.7 ElasticBox

ElasticBox is the management software that enables applications to be portable and executable to determine if the underlying infrastructure is a public or private cloud. It was founded in 2011 by Ravi Srivatsav, a senior engineer and product manager at IBM and Microsoft. Alberto Arias Maestro is another co-founder of this company, who was the previous chief architect of DynamicOps. Meanwhile, DynamicOps was purchased by VMware to serve as the fundamental part of the company's multi-cloud providing toolkit. Timothy Stephan is the executive product manager, who was a former product manager at mobile device management company MobileIron. Sierra Ventures, Andreessen Horowitz, Intel Capital, Nexus Venture Partners, AngelPad, and Raymond Tonsing are the investors in ElasticBox. Additionally, the company has an active page in Facebook to upload some photos (e.g., photos of the team members) with a life-size cardboard cut-out from David Hasselhoff. ElasticBox's core belief is that many people are working with application management through infrastructure management. This company takes a different form to allow organizations to manage and control their applications according to the infrastructure represented below.

ElasticBox uses some charts to analyze an environment and capture relevant architecture data. It obtains all the scripts necessary to install applications in the cloud and analyze all relationships with other existing services (e.g., databases and operating systems). Meanwhile, it captures all the information required to run on a diverse number of different infrastructures. This process is similar to putting the logo pieces together. The procedure carried out by the company eliminates the need for operational professionals to spend hours for fine-tuning the infrastructure. In contrast, the same cloud application can run on a large number of underlying infrastructures with the ElasticBox method when it is in the box. Note that the boxes are not just Linux containers. Through this process, various client automation tools (e.g., Puppet and Chef) still work in the cloud application. ElasticBox enables business customers and Web 2.0 to create standardized, automated, and repeatable application deployment plans. Furthermore, it can be carefully positioned to perform services as a neutral intermediary in the cloud. This process is done by supporting automation of application deployment and other technologies in a multitude of environments, from traditional data centers to public and private clouds. The founders of ElasticBox say the platform is best suited to perform development operations and test environments where an application is required to expand in the public cloud. It makes multiple applications portable on different cloud service providers. In addition, this company supports Amazon Web Services, Windows Azure, HP and Rackspace along with VMware vSphere and OpenStack based private clouds.

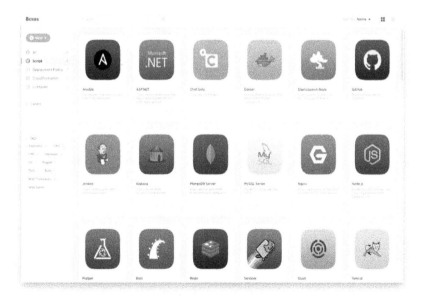

8.8 Jelastic

Jelastic is a cloud software platform to run on bare servers or virtualized data servers to create a cloud server. This is done to monitor the cloud infrastructure, quickly and easily, according to the main requirements of the application running on the server. This company hopes to be a pioneer in the idea of a platform as infrastructure. Jelastic was founded in 2011, so Ruslan Synytsky and Alexey Skutin are the co-founders of the company. Ruslan Synytsky was one of the software architecture and engineering teams at iQueLab, SolovatSoft, and Datamesh. The company is bought by John Derrick, who had considerable experiences in advising and growing new companies. Maxfield Capital, Runa Capital and Almaz Capital are the investors of this company. Ruslan Synytsky was an engineer and programmer for the National Space Agency of Ukraine. There is a trend to implement the IaaS and PaaS models. IaaS and SaaS providers are used to extend cloud applications for their own environments. Jelastic is a company that incorporates the same notion of a converged cloud system. Instead of an IaaS or SaaS service provider to enable PaaS, the company includes PaaS features to create the applications required. Jelastic builds a cloud environment to sell a software package that can be carefully connected to an existing domain on bare or virtualized hardware. It monitors and analyzes the cloud applications that are placed in the environment. The company has an IaaS platform so that various cloud application behaviors can easily help customers.

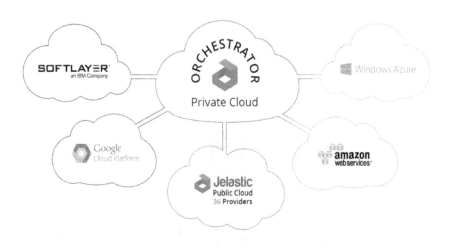

8.9 Koality

Koality's primary goal is to increase the speed requirements for code testing using cloud computing. Jonathan Chu, Jordan Potter and Brian Bland are co-founders of the company, who worked at software analytics firm Palantir Technologies. It was founded in 2012, so FF angel investor, Webb Investment Network, Felicis Venture and Index Ventures are the financial investors. The Koality title plays on the idea of code quality. The company logo is of a Koala bear hugging a repository. Developers spent much more time on building codes, which are required for many corporate companies to become the soul of their operations. The testing process is an essential part of the coding of the application to show that the code works in a real and correct way. Testing large projects can be time consuming. Additionally, it can significantly slow down the development process when testing finds no errors. This is the main problem that Koality is helping to solve in order to use the power of an elastically scalable cloud infrastructure to perform resolution operations. The main objective of the founders is to change the development process of the coding process to make it much more efficient. Developers use the code that is created and run most times on many VMs in the cloud environment, all at once. This process causes many tests to be performed in a short time. The company's trading platform uses the parallelization process to run multiple tests individually one after the other. The proxy system is another important part of Koality that investigates any tests for bugs and errors. It causes the developers of any code to be altered by various problems occurred. The Koality software platform is placed beyond a system firewall application and uses a virtual private cloud on Amazon Web Services to run tests with high computing power. All testing and coding steps are performed in secure environments.

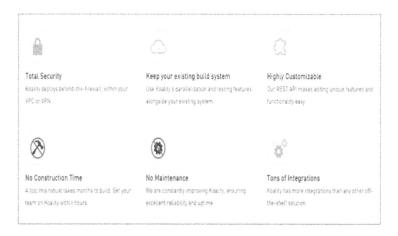

Total Security
Koality deploys behind-the-firewall, within your VPC or VPN

Keep your existing build system
Use Koality's parallelization and testing features alongside your existing system

Highly Customizable
Our REST API makes adding unique features and functionality easy

No Construction Time
A tool this robust takes months to build. Get your team on Koality within hours.

No Maintenance
We are constantly improving Koality, ensuring excellent reliability, and uptime

Tons of Integrations
Koality has more integrations than any other off-the-shelf solution.

8.10 nCrypted Cloud

nCrypted Cloud is a company that provides a platform to encrypt various files stored in consumer cloud services such as Box, DropBox, and Google Drive. Nick Stamos is the founder of this company, who was the manager of Phase Forward, which is a healthcare IT company bought by Oracle. He was also the founder of Verdasys security company and the president of this company until 2011. Additionally, the founder Igor Odnovorov worked at Phase Forward and Verdasys. nCrypted Cloud was founded in 2012, as well as the executives of Former Cisco and Microsoft are its investors. Nick Stamos accomplished a consulting work in 2012 after eight years of Verdasys establishment. This company offers data loss prevention and some of the potential encryption services for enterprise uses. Stamos built nCrypted Cloud as a company after he received the hacking information related to one of the DropBox accounts. The company-provided platform encrypts any file stored on popular cloud storage services such as DropBox, Google Drive, Box, and Microsoft Sky Drive. In addition, it offers an IT department to show employees that they stay in the clouds. The company focused on offering a Freemium-based cloud service to consumers in the first few months, but began serving healthcare and education applications. It has received less than $3 million in angel funds from previous Cisco and Microsoft executives, as well as seeking additional venture funds to scale up its activities. nCrypted Cloud provides an environment that uses a technique to place files in cloud stores in encrypted conditions using a .zip container. Subsequently, the system generates a unique authentication trigger for each client that can be automatically authorized through native nCrypted compliant applications. There is no additional password for the end user to remember different platforms to login. Therefore, customers see a new padlock icon so that they can be informed that their files have been carefully protected by nCrypted. Moreover, business customers can easily see what files and documents are stored on cloud storage platforms. nCrypted Cloud provides a platform for companies so that their employees can continue to use these systems securely.

8.11 PernixData

PernixData provides a platform that focuses on flash virtualization. It was founded by Poojan Kumar, who was the data products manager at VMware in 2012. Satyam Vaghani is the co-founder of the company, who was a chief engineer and storage manager at VMware. Lightspeed Venture Partners, Mark Leslie, John Thompson, Lane Bess, Kleiner Perkins Caufield and Byers Investor are the investors of this company. Because cloud computing has become more attractive in business uses, customers are encountering some critical conditions (e.g., storage bottlenecks). Maintaining the performance of storage with private cloud and virtualization is the fundamental problem. Replacing traditional rotary storage devices with solid-state and flash drives is the primary solution to this problem. The flash hypervisor provided by this company essentially separates the storage management system from the hardware as in the computer virtualization procedure. Note that the PernixData software platform supports the capabilities of VMware. It has some plans to support additional hypervisors and runs on top of any flash storage. Therefore, the platform does not require new investments in hardware for clients to start at the server. PernixData involves a simple software installation that allows users to achieve a large increase in operating performance.

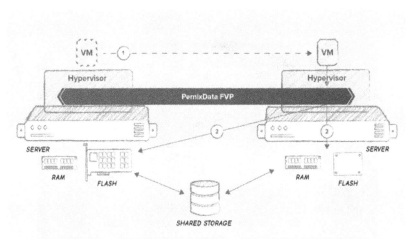

8.12 Salsify

Salsify focuses on a cloud-based product management system and some sharing skills for e-commerce websites. Jason Purcell, Jeremy Redburn and Rob Gonzalez are the co-founders of this company. They previously worked at Endeca, which was e-commerce search and navigation software purchased by Oracle in 2011. This company was founded in 2012, as well as North Bridge, Venture Partners, and Matrix Partners are its investors. Essential information about products on e-commerce websites in cloud environments is essential. E-commerce corporations can register all the products sold on their websites in the Salsify software. Therefore, the system records everything it needs to know about products for each consumer. The platform provided by Salsify makes e-commerce corporations able to provide their products on the websites. When a large number of different e-commerce corporations place their products on Salsify's cloud server, any corporation can sell the products of a partner corporation on its website by clicking on any e-commerce team. Both retailers and distributors of various products can receive data from hundreds of suppliers so they can easily confirm the information. The founders of this company say that it is not only slowing down the sales process but it is also accelerating e-commerce. Keep in mind that Salsify involves a central piece of the cloud infrastructure to enable transactions in the world of electronic commerce.

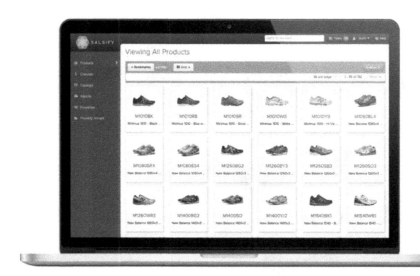

CONCLUSIONS

Cloud computing provides a scalable infrastructure for various applications, data, and files. It includes a large set of different systems that are connected in public, private and hybrid networks. Cloud technology reduces the cost of computing, makes file hosting easier, and reduces response time to user requests. The basic concepts of cloud computing come from the traditional concepts of grid computing, utility computing, and distributed computing. Cloud-based systems offer diverse capabilities through three service models, including Infrastructure as a Service (IaaS), Platform as a Service (PaaS), and Software as a Service (SaaS).

This book introduced the main concepts of cloud computing. It involves a brief introduction, various architectures, different applications, consumer platforms, primary uses, security issues, simulation tools, and some of the cloud service providers. The introduction to cloud computing was explained by the basic definition, the popularity feature, the roots, the general features, the special features, the IT foundation, the main risks and the political implications of cloud technology with the help of some concepts, such as the migration of mainframe to the cloud, web services and grid computing. Cloud computing architectures were described in various deployment models (i.e., public, private, hybrid, and community clouds) and different service models (i.e., IaaS, PaaS, and SaaS). File storage, cloud database, CRM, email, and website hosting are some important applications of cloud-based systems that were carefully described in context. Some cloud systems may implement consumer applications, such as Evernote, iCloud, and Spotify. The main uses of cloud systems in real-world domains include education, monitoring, healthcare, library, and banking. The different security concerns of cloud computing were described in this book through seven categories including security, privacy, reliability, legal issues, open standard, compliance, freedom, long-term viability, and data ownership. Subsequently, simulation tools for cloud computing (e.g., CloudSim, Xen hypervisor, and UEC) were introduced, which are used to perform the testing phase of various applications. Finally, some dominant companies that offer cloud servers worldwide (e.g., CloudLock, CloudMunch, and CloudPhysics) were considered in context. They interact with different users, including ordinary people, researchers and various companies, anytime, anywhere.

REFERENCES

1. P. Barham, B. Dragovic, K. Fraser, S. Hand, T. Harris, A. Ho, R. Neugebauer, I. Pratt, and A. Warfield. Xen and the art of virtualization. ACM SIGOPS Operating Systems Review, 2003, Vol. 37, No. 5, pp. 164–177.
2. J. Carolan, S. Gaede, J. Baty, G. Brunette, A. Licht, J. Remmell, L. Tucker, and J. Weise. Introduction to cloud computing architecture. White Paper, 1st edn. Sun Micro Systems Inc, 2009.
3. L. M. Kaufman. Data security in the world of cloud computing. IEEE Security & Privacy, 2009, Vol. 7, No. 4, pp. 61–64.
4. M. R. Goldner. Winds of change: libraries and cloud computing. BIBLIOTHEK Forschung und Praxis, 2010, Vol. 34, No. 3, pp. 270–275.
5. N. Sclater. eLearning in the Cloud. International Journal of Virtual and Personal Learning Environments, 2010, Vol. 1, No. 1, pp. 10–19.
6. R. N. Calheiros, R. Ranjan, A. Beloglazov, C. A. De Rose, and R. Buyya. CloudSim: a toolkit for the modeling and simulation of cloud resource management and application provisioning techniques. Journal of Software: Practice and Experience, 2010, Vol. 41, No. 1, pp. 23–50.
7. R. Buyya, J. Broberg, and A. M. Goscinski. Cloud computing: principles and paradigms. John Wiley & Sons, 2010, Vol. 87.
8. D. Johnson, K. Murari, M. Raju, R. Suseendran, and Y. Girikumar. Eucalyptus beginner's guide-uec edition. Ubuntu Server, 2010.
9. M. Armbrust, A. Fox, R. Griffith, A. D. Joseph, R. Katz, A. Konwinski, G. Lee, D. Patterson, A. Rabkin, and I. Stoica. A view of cloud computing. Communications of the ACM, 2010, Vol. 53, No. 4, pp. 50–58.

10. A. B. Letaifa, A. Haji, M. Jebalia, and S. Tabbane. State of the Art and Research Challenges of new services architecture technologies: Virtualization, SOA and Cloud Computing. International Journal of Grid and Distributed Computing, 2010, Vol. 3, No. 4, pp. 69–88.

11. N. M. M. K. Chowdhury and R. Boutaba. A survey of network virtualization. Computer Networks, 2010, Vol. 54, No. 5, pp. 862–876.

12. V. J. R. Winkler. Securing the Cloud: Cloud computer Security techniques and tactics. Elsevier, 2011.

13. J. Spring. Monitoring cloud computing by layer, part 1. IEEE Security & Privacy, 2011, Vol. 9, No. 2, pp. 66–68.

14. J. Spring. Monitoring cloud computing by layer, part 2. IEEE Security & Privacy, 2011, Vol. 9, No. 3, pp. 52–55.

15. S. M. Fulton. 16 December 2011. Available on URL: http://www.readwrite.com.

16. D. Zissis and D. Lekkas. Addressing cloud computing security issues. Future Generation Computer Systems, 2012, Vol. 28, No. 3, pp. 583–592.

17. K. Jackson. OpenStack cloud computing cookbook. Packt Publishing Ltd, 2012.

ABOUT THE AUTHOR

Mohammad Samadi Gharajeh received ASc in Computer Software in 2005, BSc in Engineering of Computer Software Technology in 2009, and MSc in Computer Engineering – Computer Systems Architecture in 2013. He has already developed various software systems, simulations, intelligent systems, and research projects. His research interests include distributed systems, cloud computing, wireless sensor networks, software systems, and artificial intelligence. He was a member of the Technical Program Committee and Reviewer in some of the international conference proceedings. In addition, he is a member of the Editorial Board and Reviewer in some of the international scientific journals, a Lecturer of university, an IEEE Member, and an IAENG Member now.

www.ingramcontent.com/pod-product-compliance
Lightning Source LLC
Chambersburg PA
CBHW071225050326
40689CB00011B/2457